Map from the *Handy Railroad Atlas* © 1948 by Rand McNally R.L. 93-S-103.

A History
of Railroading
in Western North Carolina

Cary Franklin Poole

The Overmountain Press
JOHNSON CITY, TENNESSEE

ISBN 0-932807-87-9

2 3 4 5 6 7 8 9 0

CONTENTS

DEDICATION, ACKNOWLEDGMENTS, AND THANKS

This volume is dedicated first to my father, Frank Poole, who spent his entire working career with the railroad. He began his career with the Central of Georgia, then worked with the Southern, and concluded his career with the Norfolk Southern Corporation. Without him, I would not have the appreciation of the history and the importance of the railroad industry.

This volume is also dedicated to my mother, Mary Poole, who not only had to deal with a career railroad man, but also had to deal with a son who is a dyed-in-the-wool railfan.

And lastly, I dedicate this volume to my wife, Carole, who tolerates the railfanning, listens to the exploits, and, above all, appreciates a husband's hobby. Hopefully she understands this hobby contributes not only to the recording of a particular piece of history, but keeps a husband busy with something he loves.

I would like to acknowledge four individuals who have contributed to this publication on almost a weekly basis. Those four are:

M. B. (Mac) Connery, who had the patience to guide and instruct and who opened up his house and darkroom skills to someone unknown in the fields of photography and railroad research. Mac was kind enough to direct me in my searches for material through his numerous contacts. He was also a constant source of encouragement.

David LeNoir, who has served as copy editor for this volume. There has been a constant stream of correspondence and packages shuttling between Mars Hill, North Carolina, and Spearfish, South Dakota. I appreciate David for taking time from his busy teaching schedule to help with the proofreading and copy editing.

Tom L. Sink was the first individual to encourage me with the idea of this volume. Tom was the proprietor of a model shop in Asheville, North Carolina, and it was there the need for such a volume became evident from the customers' input. Tom also was instrumental in introducing me to key people who later contributed to the manuscript. I feel few people know railroad prototypes as does Tom L.

Sink. Many of the fine action photographs came from the negative collection he has compiled over the years.

And Doug Walker. To put it simply, he served as the "eastern arm" for this research project. He contributed the article on the Carolina & North-Western, rounded up photographs, and kept my spirits up when lulls appeared.

There are several people I would like to thank for their contributions to this publication. Thanks to:

Frank Ardrey of Birmingham, Alabama, for the wonderful photographs of the Southern Railway and the short lines in Western North Carolina.

Dale Roberts of Spartanburg, South Carolina, had a unique opportunity to photograph the F-units around Asheville, North Carolina, as a teenager, and I thank him for sharing the photographs.

Glover Machine Works for opening up their files of the locomotives built by their corporation. And to Dick Hillman of the Georgia Northeastern Railroad for preserving the glass negatives of the Glover Machine Works and allowing me access to the prints.

Lee Medford of Altapass, North Carolina. It was a cold day we spent in his caboose, but well worth the experience to hear of his days either working on some of the narrow gauge lines or as a salvage dealer cleaning up Clinchfield wrecks. I have since learned of Mr. Medford's passing; he will be sorely missed.

Harold K. Vollrath for his contributions on several of the short lines in Western North Carolina.

Richard Watts, curator of the Canton Area Historical Museum, for helping with leads and information on the Champion Paper Company.

The Great Smoky Mountain Railroad and Trainmaster John Norcross. Both the Great Smoky Mountain Railroad and John have been extremely helpful in providing information on the history of the Murphy Branch of the Southern Railway.

Ray Rapp, my sidekick on many field trips and, more importantly, originator of the "Whistlestops in Western North Carolina" program. This program has become a staple in the Mars Hill College Elderhostel offerings and was a direct reason for compiling and publishing this volume.

John Campbell of Mars Hill College. John had the patience to show me the ways of the darkroom. He crammed a semester's photography class into only a few hours, and some of the prints in the manuscript illustrate his expertise. John was also instrumental in helping to develop the slide show which I used in promoting the publication.

Rodney Snedeker and the U.S. Forest Service for providing leads and photographs from their collections.

Jim King for his assistance in providing much valued information on the Southern Railway and the Graham County Railroad. Jim also pointed me to other individuals who provided even more material.

Bruce Sprinkle of Grapevine, North Carolina, who was instrumental in locating material in Madison County.

Jerry Ledford for his help in locating many of the logging photographs.

Jody Higgins of the Yancey County *Common Times*. Jody was instrumental in allowing me access to information which added tremendously to the chapter on the Black Mountain Railroad and the associated logging operations.

Bill Barnes and Terry Sichta of the Georgia Institute of Technology. These two gentlemen provided information on the Glover Machine Works Company of Marietta, Georgia.

Tom Fetters for the logging railroad maps. Tom is forthcoming on a history of logging activity in Western North Carolina, North Georgia, and East Tennessee.

Brian Koontz for creating the artwork used on the dust jacket cover. This is Brian's first cover, and I thank him for allowing me to use the work for this publication.

C. K. Marsh and Tom King, who helped tie together some loose ends.

The following institutions have provided research and information for this manuscript: Mars Hill College; Western Carolina University; the Presbyterian Historical Foundation; Pack Memorial Library of Asheville, North Carolina; the *Common Times* of Burnsville, North Carolina; the *Transylvania Times* of Brevard, North Carolina; and the Ramsey Library of the University of North Carolina at Asheville.

INTRODUCTION

When I "toyed" with the prospect of writing the history of railroading in Western North Carolina, I was prompted by three major factors. First and foremost, an Elderhostel program titled "Whistlestops in Western North Carolina," developed by Ray Rapp at Mars Hill College, was the primary reason for my initial interest in the region's rail history. The inaugural program was a tremendous success, and the program continues to be a staple in the Elderhostel schedule at Mars Hill College.

The second reason, in a sense, springboarded from the first. While preparing lectures for the Elderhostel program, I soon became aware how interested others were in our regional history. It was also apparent that little research in modern times had been completed on the historical development of the railroads in Western North Carolina. The local residents were also interested in their own history, and they provided much information which filled in many of the gaps. And so a need arose to detail, describe, and document the regional history as best I could.

And lastly, good friends such as Tom L. Sink, Mac Connery, and Ray Rapp strongly urged me to put to paper the railroad history of Western North Carolina. When you have friends pointing you in the right directions, providing leads, and introducing you to key contacts, it accelerates the ease in which the project goes together. Without the direction and input of these good friends, the volume could not have been produced.

Some readers will observe from skimming through this volume that every railroad in Western North Carolina is not included. One volume could not document every single rail operation which occurred in this region. The regional history is simply that rich.

One aspect of railroad development I wanted to include was the development of the Class 1 railroads. The two main lines which are included are the Southern and the Clinchfield railroads, and you cannot ignore their importance to the area. The Southern is included because of its rich history of incorporating many of the region's short lines. The Clinchfield Railroad is included due to its convo-

luted history in which it went through several ownerships and encountered many problems, including incorporating several disjointed sections of track between Elkhorn City, Kentucky, and Spartanburg, South Carolina. These two railroads, while currently partners of major rail mergers, enjoy some of the most ardent and loyal followings of any railroads in the country. Their railfans know the history, the peculiarities, and the operations of each of the respective railroads.

A good reason for including short lines, and logging railroads, was their association or connection with one of the above mentioned main line railroads. While every short line could not be included, it was my intent to include as many of the short lines which radiated from the main lines as possible. The decision to include short lines that shared these connections with the Southern or the Clinchfield only helped to illustrate the regional history and to document the economic development of the area.

While sending out 150+ pieces of correspondence to individuals, institutions, clubs, and newspapers, I realized the availability of photographs would dictate the direction the publication would take. From the individuals who responded, the generosity was overwhelming. Some could only produce a single photograph or a single story, but collectively the history of the region began to emerge.

One phenomenon materialized which I had not counted on from the local residents. Many mountain people are often stereotyped as not being extremely hospitable with "outsiders." I found this to be largely untrue. In fact, once I had established myself and had earned their confidence, I found many of the locals had an intense interest in the regional history and were quite willing to have the history recorded. A wealth of stories of kin working on the railroads, with logging operations, or in the sawmills was told to me whenever I could find the time to listen. The art of storytelling and the passing of oral histories to the next generation is not a lost art in Western North Carolina. For this reason, I was determined to incorporate as much of the local color as I could.

The basic premise I tried to follow was to incorporate a basic history of each of the railroads included within the manuscript. Each railroad was documented from the original incorporation, chartering, or inception through the course of its corporate history. I took the history through to the railroad's demise as a viable carrier or, in some cases, to its current operation as a functioning railroad.

The history of the area in many cases demonstrated a cycle which occurs in railroad development. Short lines emerged during the rapid railroad building of the 1880s and were absorbed by the larger railroads after the turn of the century. However, lately the trend has been exactly the opposite—large railroads are casting off unprofitable branches, and these are once again becoming short line operations. The Carolina & Northwestern, the

original line for the Marietta & North Georgia, and the Black Mountain railroads represent this new trend. Without the high cost of state-of-the-art locomotive power, union wages, and crew size mandates, the short lines are indeed making a comeback in the 1980s and 1990s.

And lastly, a fault I found with earlier volumes regarding railroads was the lack of a map which covered the areas traversed by the railroad in question. Most short lines had a simple set of termini, where the railroad would originate at one and finish at another. It was my hope to include at least a simple map for each railroad and include the communities served by that railroad. In this manner, the community pride which contributed to this volume can be visualized and fond remembrances of "their" railroad can be rekindled.

SOUTHERN RAILWAY, AFFILIATED LINES, AND ACQUISITIONS

The turnpike was once the only form of transportation through many of the counties of Western North Carolina. Collection of Bruce Sprinkle.

Wreck of the 252

Tell me friends, what would you do if you had been on 252?

Listen up folks if you'd like to hear about a runaway train and its engineer, one called 252, when gears down in the engine blew.

It was on that Southern Railway line, Balsom depot, Carolina. Sam Fran was the engineer, he sang a song, but he ain't here.

They watched those mountains go passing by, too fast to jump, no place to hide. Tell me friends, what would you do if you had been on 252?

Was backing down that dark gray grade, to pick up a car they'd left astray when the brakes went out on 252 and the gears in the engine blew.

At the second trestle they jumped the track, three good men ain't a-coming back. Hit that curve so did they pray, on their way to the judgment day.

They watched those mountains go passing by, too fast to jump, no place to hide. Tell me friends, what would you do if you'd been on 252?

Lyrics by Thad Beach
Recorded by Bill Morris
at Ivy Creek Recordings
Mars Hill, North Carolina

The feeling of helplessness exhibited by the crew of the 252 epitomized the feelings many people shared regarding the completion of the railroad into Western North Carolina. Due to lack of capital, scandals, and the mountain barriers themselves, it was difficult for many to believe the railroad would ever be completed.

The North Carolina Railroad

The dream of a westward route linking the many regions of North Carolina started in 1851 with the formation of the North Carolina Railroad. Discussions had risen in the 1840s concerning an east-west route, and as each successive year passed, the need became more pressing and the requests for such a route became more organized.

During the General Assembly of 1848-1849 a bill was proposed to construct a railroad, using state funds to charter it with an initial capital stock of $3 million. The House vote was 60 to 52, but the Senate vote resulted in a tie. With Speaker of the Senate Calvin Graves casting a tie breaking "yea," the funding and approval was secured. Rather than being heckled for taking such a radical stance, Speaker Graves' position was cheered throughout the state as "Speaker Graves has saved the State—the railroad bill has passed."

The initial investment of $3 million was to be derived from two sources: the first million was derived from private funds, and the remaining two million was to come from state appropriations. Progress on the railroad was soon evident, and the survey for the route was completed by 1850. Actual construction on the roadbed followed in 1851. A segment of operating railroad was completed on January 29, 1856, allowing trains to travel between Goldsboro and Charlotte.

During the Civil War, the railroad, while extremely valuable for the movement of troops for the Southern cause, suffered heavily at the hands of Union invaders. After the Civil War, rebuilding the line commenced at full speed, and over 100,000 ties were replaced during the first year.

The Best Friend of Charleston as depicted on a glass negative obtained from the Railroad Museum of Pennsylvania. The Best Friend of Charleston was the first locomotive to pull a regularly scheduled passenger train. It operated on the South Carolina Canal & Rail Road Company line, which eventually became part of the Southern Railway System.

With the depression of 1891 finally over, the management of many railroads found themselves overextended as far as capital outlays and potential targets for mergers and foreclosure. J. P. Morgan, a hugely successful financier, realized in the early 1890s that several of the Southeastern railroads could be merged into a single system. With this in mind, the railroad became part of J. P. Morgan's overall consolidation plan when the Southern Railway was organized in 1894. Prior to the Southern's organization, the North Carolina Railroad was leased to the Richmond & Danville Railroad for a period of 30 years. The Richmond & Danville went into receivership and reappeared as part of the Southern's organization in 1894. In 1895 the Southern Railway leased the North Carolina Railroad for a period of 99 years. (The line has been in service for the entire period with either the Southern Railway or its successor, the Norfolk Southern Corporation. The lease is to be renegotiated by 1995.)

Western North Carolina Railroad

In 1866 a young civil engineer was selected to initiate the construction of a railroad from Salisbury to Old Fort, North Carolina. The engineer, James W. Wilson, had served as a major for the Confederacy in the Civil War. Wilson was not satisfied with the projected route, which had been surveyed prior to the war. He and Major Bomah, another civil engineer, personally inspected Old Fort Mountain and the surrounding area for an alternate route. Unsuccessful in their search, the two men concluded that the only viable route was to build the "Loops" and to keep the grade to a minimum.

The fledgling railroad was to experience several successes as well as many setbacks, including scandal. On October 15, 1869, George W. Swepson was appointed president of the Western North Carolina Railroad. The next August, the state legislature authorized Swepson to issue bonds for construction which were not to exceed $12 million. Due to pres-

An often used photograph shows a broad gauge locomotive in the Birch Ridge Cut of Western North Carolina. Courtesy of the North Carolina Archives.

sure from the new stockholders, the railroad was divided into two divisions. With legislative approval, the first division was to extend from Salisbury to Asheville, and the second division from Asheville to both Ducktown and Paint Rock, Tennessee.

North Carolina was soon rocked by scandal over the issuing of the stock and the legislatively approved divisions. Milton S. Littlefield, a supposed Maine carpetbagger, had subscribed to 2,000 of the 3,080 shares issued. Hugh Reynolds of Statesville held an additional 1,000 shares. This left absolute control of the railroad in the hands of only a couple of individuals.

Due to suspicion of misconduct, Swepson resigned his position of president, and Littlefield, the largest stockholder, assumed the presidency. On March 27, 1870, the legislature appointed a commission of five men to investigate the matter and to issue a formal report. The commission became known informally as the "Woodfin" Commission. The five commissioners selected to serve were J. L. Henry, N. W. Woodfin, W. P. Willet, W. G. Candler, and W. W. Rollins.

Upon hearing a legislative commission was to

North Carolina concedes the deaths of 120 convicts to build the Western North Carolina Railroad. Many researchers believe the number of deaths reported by the state to be far too low. Some researchers believe the number could actually exceed 400 deaths. Courtesy of the North Carolina State

investigate, both Littlefield and Swepson fled the state. They boarded a train in Raleigh and ordered the crew to travel without the headlight and marker lights illuminated. The investigation concluded that $4 million of state bonds had been endorsed and could not be fully accounted for.

This financial disaster caused the construction to stop when Major Wilson had progressed only three miles west of Old Fort. To keep the idea of a commercial route fresh in the minds of the legislators and the local residents, Wilson contracted with a stagecoach line to carry passengers the remainder of the journey from Old Fort to Asheville.

After a seven year lull, the legislature approved reorganization of the railroad with an appropriation of $880,000 in 1877. In 1878 the state furnished Wilson with 500 convicts, who, at very low maintenance costs, would help supplement the appropriations of the year before.

Major Wilson had carefully chosen the projected route. The roadbed would be an engineering miracle when finished. The linear distance from milepost 113, just west of Old Fort, to the east entrance of the Swannanoa Tunnel is only 3.4 miles. However, Wilson had to construct nine miles of ever-curving track to traverse that distance. The track contained a total of 2,776.4 degrees of curvature, the equivalent of nearly eight complete circles. While the roadbed was one part of the engineering feat, construction took into account a difference of 891 feet in elevation and the boring of seven tunnels. The nine miles of track, the curves, and the tunnels were all necessary to ensure the grade of 2.1% which Wilson required.

Although six of the seven tunnels were of relatively short length, the Swannanoa Tunnel was a challenge in its own right with a length of 1,832 feet. Construction was not the only challenge involving the tunnels. The steady grade of 2+% mandated a heavy workload for the steam engines over the completed line.

Due to the hard-working nature of the engines and the heavy traffic, exhaust from the stacks hung heavy in the tunnels. To remedy constant complaints from the crews, breathing devices were necessary for use by crew members on many of the locomotives.

A postcard of the Western North Carolina Railroad shows two trains that, while appearing to be on different tracks, are both heading westbound to Salisbury, North Carolina. Courtesy of the North Carolina State Archives.

Dusty Rhodes, an engineer on the CNO&TP, a Southern Railway subsidiary, developed a form of gas mask which the crews used for fresh air. The crews often compared the mask to a horse's feeding bag. The device was made of canvas and was connected to a hose which supplied fresh air from an intake, located under the locomotive, that could not become contaminated from the engine's exhaust.

In order to expedite the completion of the railroad into Asheville, Wilson decided to attempt boring from both entrances of the Swannanoa Tunnel simultaneously. To accomplish this feat, he felt a work crew, complete with a locomotive, was needed to help haul supplies and laborers to the work sites.

It was decided the *Salisbury*, a small 4-4-0 American which had survived the Civil War, would be

This Norris-built 4-4-0 named the *Salisbury* is shown with a work train in Western North Carolina. The locomotive was hauled by oxen and men over the Swannanoa Gap to facilitate the construction of the Swannanoa Tunnel from the west side. Collection of Harold K. Vollrath.

used in the construction between Asheville and the west port of the Swannanoa Tunnel. To accomplish the transportation of the *Salisbury*, a hand-picked labor crew and ten oxen began moving the engine over the mountain. Sections of track were laid, and as the *Salisbury* moved forward, the previously passed sections were removed and relaid in front of the locomotive. After several weeks, the crew crested the mountain and slid the locomotive down the other side on a skid.

Major Wilson was faced with the herculean task of removing solid granite obstacles from the excavation. Since the South was still viewed with a certain level of hostility and suspicion, black powder was scarce. Either the cost was too prohibitive—at 50 cents a pound when available—or it simply could not be had at any price. Wilson solved the problem of cracking layered rock by building huge pyres of pine logs as high as the convicts could stack the wood, allowing the pyres to burn down to hot coals, and then having the convicts pour buckets of cold water onto the rocks. The cold water caused a sudden contraction in the layered rock formations, making the rock crack. The process was extremely

slow, but the labor was cheap and the area offered a seemingly inexhaustible supply of wood.

Some blasting, however, was utilized. Steel-tipped bars were driven into the solid rock by sledgehammers to facilitate boring for blasting holes. Most holes were hammered as deep as possible, usually no deeper than two feet. Once drilled, a blasting mixture was tamped into the hole. With black powder being both scarce and expensive, nitroglycerine and cornmeal, mixed into a paste to aid in the handling of the high explosive, was tamped into the drill hole. Primed reeds or elder tubes were inserted into the mixture to serve as an ignition fuse. The crews made a line of pine needles which led away from the drill hole. By lighting the line of needles, the crews gained a few additional seconds in order to reach safety.

Because poorly trained convicts were handling the explosives, many deaths resulted from the improper handling of the charges. North Carolina recognizes the deaths of 120 convicts, but researchers fear the figure could be as high as 400. Since the bulk of the convicts ranged from robbers

A cancelled postcard depicts the Old Fort Loops on the Western North Carolina Railroad with Andrews Geyser in the lower left-hand corner. Courtesy of the North Carolina Archives.

A work train in Mud Cut on Southern Railway's mainline between Asheville and Salisbury, North Carolina, circa 1900. Courtesy of the Austin-Brooks Collection, Ramsey Library, UNC-Asheville.

to murderers, little or no notice was given to their deaths by the state.

Rebecca Harding Davis, a traveler who visited Western North Carolina in the late 1870s, described the conditions of the labor camps in poignant detail. She states, "the gorge swarmed with hundreds of wretched blacks in the striped yellow convict garb. After their supper was cooked (over campfires) and eaten, they were driven into a row of prison cars, where they were tightly boxed for the night, with no possible chance to obtain either air or light." The conditions in the camps were squalid and horrifying, the work backbreaking, and if a prisoner died, he was buried beside the tracks with no ceremony. The work simply continued.

The Swannanoa Tunnel was completed on March 11, 1879. Major Wilson met Major Troy, chief engineer, in the center of the tunnel, a length of 1,832 feet cut through solid rock. Chief Engineer Troy sent a message to Governor Zebulan Vance, a Western North Carolina native. The telegram read, "Daylight entered Buncombe County today through the Swannanoa Tunnel. Grades and center met exactly." Little else needed to be said, for the resi-

A passenger train is photographed in Mud Cut between Old Fort and Black Mountain, North Carolina, circa 1900. Courtesy of the Austin-Brooks Collection, Ramsey Library, UNC-Asheville.

dents of Western North Carolina finally were connected politically and economically through a mode of transportation with the rest of the state.

The celebration concerning the completion of the Swannanoa Tunnel was short-lived, however. Shortly after the telegram was sent to Governor Vance, the locomotive *Salisbury* was backing out of the tunnel with a flatcar carrying 23 convict laborers. A cave-in occured, and all of the convicts died from the falling debris.

Despite Major Wilson's success, the state decided to sell the railroad at public auction to the highest bidder. On April 27, 1880, the railroad was sold to William J. Best and his associates with the stipulation that three legislative requirements were met. The requirements were:

1) The extension from Asheville to Paint Rock, Tennessee, would be completed before July 1, 1881. The Ducktown, Tennessee, extension from Asheville was to be completed by January 1, 1885.

2) The new owners would repay in full amount

A postcard labeled "On Line of the Southern Railroad" depicts a locomotive rounding Andrews Geyser. Courtesy of the North Carolina State Archives.

Southern #2028, an Alco RS-3, pulls a string of cars on the old "Peavine" section of track formerly owned by the Triple C Railroad. Photograph by J.H. Wade. Collection of Frank Ardrey.

Number 5059, a 2-10-2, emerges from the Swannanoa Tunnel with pusher #5074 in the rear. The date is July 4, 1948. Collection of Frank Ardrey.

all money paid by the railroad construction which had been spent between March 29 and April 27, 1880, the date of the sale.

3) The labor of the 500 convicts was to be paid at an annual rate of $125 per convict to the state.

William Best, the new owner of the Western North Carolina Railroad, became an agent of the Richmond & Danville Railroad, and those two railroads later merged to form the East Tennessee, Virginia & Georgia Railroad. This system allowed North Carolina to become connected with East Tennessee through the junction at Paint Rock, Tennessee. However, with the rise and fall of railroad fortunes, the entire system entered bankruptcy on June 15, 1892.

Shortly before the bankruptcy, the Western North Carolina Railroad was able to fulfill all of the legislative provisions called for in the bill of sale to William Best, except for the time schedules. The connection from central North Carolina to East Tennessee, the line to Paint Rock, was completed in 1881, only a year behind schedule. The extension to

Western North Carolina Railroad #25 moves a string of cars over a trestle near the French Broad River. Courtesy of the North Carolina State Archives.

Ducktown, Tennessee, progressed westward, reaching Canton in 1882, Waynesville in 1883, and Murphy in 1891. The extension into Ducktown was never completed, and Murphy remained the western terminus for the railroad.

The Western North Carolina Railroad had been in a hotly contested race with the Louisville & Nashville Railroad for entry into Ducktown. After financial setbacks, scandal, and even poor advice on laying the roadbed through the Nantahala Gorge, the Richmond & Danville Railroad (successor to the Western North Carolina Railroad) had been beaten in the race. Both railroads viewed the developing copper mining activity in the area of Ducktown as a lucrative way to increase traffic revenues.

When the ETV&G and the R&D entered receivership in June 1892, the complete railroad system caught the eye of three men who later became the appointed receivers. The three men were Fred W. Huidekoper, Samuel Spencer, and Reuben Foster—all of whom were instrumental in the initial founding of the Southern Railway system and the merging of the R&D into that system.

A Western North Carolina 4-4-0 American pulls a string of Civil War vintage coaches through Morganton, North Carolina. The photograph was taken in the 1870s. Collection of Doug Walker.

On August 22, 1894, the Richmond & Danville Railroad was officially merged into the Southern Railway system. The Western North Carolina Railroad became a part of the Southern system on Sep-

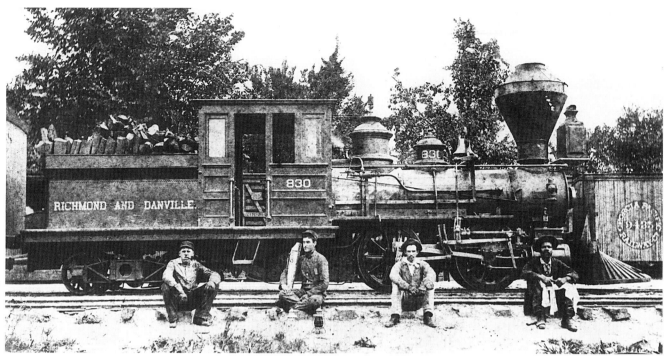

A Richmond & Danville 0-4-4 Forney is photographed in Morganton, North Carolina. Collection of Doug Walker.

726 R&D — RICHMOND & DANVILLE RAILROAD COMPANY.
(PIEDMONT AIR-LINE)
WESTERN NORTH CAROLINA DIVISION.

SALISBURY AND PAINT ROCK.

No. 11	Ml	*November* 20, 1892.	No. 12
		LEAVE] [ARRIVE	
*11 10 A.M.	0	+...Salisbury.....ठ	8 37 P.M.
11 38 "	14	.. ...Cleveland ....ठ	8 12 "
11 48 A.M.	19	......Elmwood......	8 02 "
12 03 NO'N	26	+.....Statesville...ठ	7 47 "
12 29 "	39	.....Catawba.....ठ	7 19 "
12 38 ▼	42	.....Claremont.....	7 08 "
12 48 "	48	+.....Newton.....ठ	6 56 "
12 53 NO'N	50	......Conover.. ...	6 51 "
1 09 P.M.	58	+.....Hickory.....ठ	6 35 "
1 30 "	68	..Connelly's Springs.ठ	5 56 "
1 52 "	79	+ ...Morganton...ठ	5 33 "
2 04 "	85	......Glen Alpine	5 21 "
2 14 "	90	......Bridgewater...ठ	5 11 "
2 24 "	94	........Nebo.	5 01 "
2 36 "	100	........Marion.....ठ	4 49 "
2 47 "	105	. ....Greenlee.....	4 35 "
2 58 "	112	......Old Fort.....ठ	4 21 "
3 14 "	116	....Round Knob....	4 08 "
3 48 "	126	....Black Mountain..ठ	3 37 "
3 53 "	130	.......Cooper's...ठ	3 23 "
4 18 "	139	......Biltmore....ठ	2 55 "
4 25 "	142	arr.+.Asheville ठ .lve.	2 45 "
4 33 "	142	lve..Asheville...arr.	12 20 "
4 49 "	148	........Olivette.....	1 59 "
4 59 "	153	......Alexander ....ठ	1 49 "
5 23 "	164	. ....Marshall.....ठ	1 22 "
5 39 "	171	......Barnard.....	1 02 P.M.
5 45 "	174	....Sandy Bottom....	12 53 NO'N
5 57 "	180	+....Hot Springs...ठ	12 39 "
6 10 P.M.	186	+...Paint Rock.....	*12 25 NO'N
		ARRIVE] [LEAVE	

ASHEVILLE AND MURPHY.

No. 17	Ml	*November* 20, 1892.	No. 18
		LEAVE] [ARRIVE	
†8 30 A.M.	0	+..Asheville...ठ	2 35 P.M.
8 39 "	2	......Emma.....	2 23 "
8 48 "	5	.. Sulphur Springs..	2 14 "
9 02 "	9	......Hominy.....	2 00 "
9 20 "	14	......Turnpike.....	1 41 "
9 37 "	18	......Canton......	1 24 "
9 49 "	23	.......Clyde......	1 12 P.M.
10 29 "	28	....Waynesville.ठ	12 52 NO'N
10 32 "	36	....Balsam.....	12 25 NO'N
10 55 "	41	.......Hall......	11 56 A.M.
11 10 "	43	.......Addie.....	11 45 "
11 27 "	47	.....Sylva....ठ	11 27 "
11 33 "	49	....Dillsboro...ठ	11 21 "
11 57 A.M.	55	......Wilmot.....	10 57 "
12 13 NO'N	59	.....Whittier.....	10 41 "
1 09 P.M.	65	....Bryson City.ठ	10 15 "
2 22 "	84	......Almond...ठ	8 47 "
2 57 "	94	......Hewitt.....	8 12 "
3 06 "	96	....Nantahala...ठ	8 02 "
3 53 "	103	......Rhodo....ठ	7 21 "
4 09 "	108	....Andrews...ठ	‖7 05 "
4 39 "	118	....Tomotla....	6 20 "
5 09 P.M.	124	....Murphy.....	†6 00 A.M.
		ARRIVE] [LEAVE	

SPARTANBURG AND ASHEVILLE.

No. 13	M	*November* 20, 1892.	M	No. 14
		LRAVE] [ARRIVE		
*6 50 P.M.	0	+.Spartanburg.ठ	70	10 15 A.M.
7 16 "	10	.....Campton.....	6c	9 47 "
7 23 "	12	......Inman.....ठ	58	9 40 "
7 37 "	18	....Campobella...ठ	52	9 26 "
7 48 "	23	... ..Landrum....	47	9 1? "
7 58 "	27	......Tryon......ठ	43	9 06 "
8 15 "	33	......Melrose......	37	8 52 "
8 27 "	37	......Saluda.. .ठ	33	8 37 "
8 38 "	40	......Zirconia.....	30	8 2? "
8 54 "	45	......Flat Rock.....	25	8 12 "
9 05 "	48	+..Hendersonville.ठ	22	8 02 "
9 15 "	52	......Hillgirt.....	18	7 53 "
9 26 "	56	......Fletcher's......	14	7 42 "
9 34 "	59	......Arden......	11	7 35 "
9 40 "	60	......Skyland.... ..	10	7 30 "
9 44 "	61	......Busbee.....	9	7 27 "
10 00 "	68	......Biltmore....ठ	2	7 10 "
10 10 P.M.	70	+..Asheville...ठ	0	*7 00 A.M.
		ARRIVE] [LEAVE		

N.B.—Trains marked * run daily ; †daily, except Sunday : ‖meals. + Coupon stations; ठ Telegraph stations.

For other Connections to ASHEVILLE AND HOT SPRINGS all the year round resorts, see page 721.

The shortlived Richmond & Danville Railroad in Western North Carolina was preceded by the Western North Carolina Railroad and followed by the newly formed Southern Railway. Courtesy of *The Official Railway Guide.*

A Western North Carolina Railroad locomotive pulls a train across the upper tier of the loop near Dendron, North Carolina. Courtesy of the North Carolina State Archives.

tember 1, 1894, and a long-time proponent, Colonel Alexander B. Andrews, became the first vice president of the Southern Railway.

Along with Major Wilson, Colonel Andrews is recognized as being one of the most ardent supporters of the Western North Carolina Railroad. He had served as a civil engineer with the Raleigh & Gaston Railroad. Upon his employment with the Western North Carolina Railroad, he was directly responsi-

Southern locomotive #1491 pulls a passenger train into Ridgecrest, North Carolina, during September 1938. Photograph by W.H. Thrall. Collection of Frank Ardrey.

Ts-1 class #1479, a 4-8-2, is photographed near Ridgecrest, North Carolina, on September 13, 1938. Photograph by W.H. Thrall. Collection of Frank Ardrey.

ble for the construction of the line from Asheville to Paint Rock, Tennessee, and later for the construction on the Murphy Branch.

Asheville & Spartanburg Railroad

As Major Wilson and Colonel Andrews were struggling to complete the WNC Railroad into Asheville and points beyond, a second railroad was attempting to reach Asheville, in this case from the south. Governor Zebulon Vance, a native of the Western North Carolina area, and his South Carolina gubernatorial counterpart, Robert Hayne (for whom Hayne Shop of the Southern Railway in Spartanburg is named), promoted a route from Spartanburg to Asheville and points north.

The charter for this particular route was granted to the Greenville & French Broad Railroad in 1855, the same approximate date of incorporation of the North Carolina Railroad, parent company of its counterpart in the race to Asheville. In 1859 the engineers' report was released, estimating over $2 million to construct the line over four operating divisions. The costs per division were:

SC Division	$477,496
Tryon Division	804,293
Green River Division	375,726
Upper French Broad Division	474,763
Total cost for 79 miles	$2,132,278

With a price tag of over $2 million, little interest was stimulated in the project and only speculation could be made as to whether the money could be raised. The issue was temporarily postponed when General Pierre Beauregard opened fire on Fort Sumter in the spring of 1861.

The Spartanburg & Asheville Railroad was chartered in 1873, and construction commenced in 1876. The railroad soon encountered financial difficulties and was placed into receivership. It was reorganized as the Asheville & Spartanburg Railroad in 1881.

As the Western North Carolina Railroad had Major Wilson as a capable engineer, the Asheville & Spartanburg Railroad found as his equal Captain Charles W. Pearson. Pearson, a Confederate officer, helped survey the surrounding area and helped to determine the route.

Pearson found the railroad floundering only 26 miles out of Spartanburg and experiencing successive bouts of financial troubles. Unlike his counterpart, Major Wilson, who was fortunate to have located relatively gentle foothills, Pearson encountered an almost sheer wall of rock in the form of Saluda Mountain. Combined with a lack of an alternative route and a lack of funding to lay tracks around the mountain, the Asheville & Spartanburg Railroad lost the race into Asheville to the Western North Carolina Railroad on March 11, 1879.

The A&S line crept toward Asheville at what the residents of Buncombe County believed to be a snail's pace. The line reached Tryon, North Carolina, by early 1878, but it was the geography just north of Tryon that stalled further construction as the survey crews desperately searched for a route which would incorporate a gentle grade rather than going up and over Saluda Mountain.

Captain Pearson conducted the survey with Colonel Thad Coleman, just recently released from the employment of the Western North Carolina Railroad. With the completion of its route up to the Swannanoa Tunnel, the Western North Carolina

Railroad had released some of its engineers and laborers from employment. The two engineers were faced with the choice of two routes. The first involved building up and over Saluda Mountain at a grade percentage twice the normally accepted practice of 2%. The other route involved the boring of tunnels, at least 13 additional miles of track, and the prospect of dealing with shifting sand formations.

With the lack of financing ever critical, the two engineers chose the former route and proceeded north of Tryon with the intention of constructing track up and over Saluda Mountain. The first train reached the summit of Saluda on July 4, 1878. To ensure a second route into Asheville, the state legislature and Buncombe County issued bonds to complete the line. Buncombe County alone issued a bond of $100,000 to help finance the railroad into Asheville. With the assistance from North Carolina and Buncombe County, the railroad reached Hendersonville by June 1879. A bill was introduced into the North Carolina legislature to forfeit the charter of the railroad if construction did not assume a faster pace. The bill, coincidently, was introduced by Richard Pearson, a relative of Charles Pearson,

Southern #1464, a Ts 4-8-2, on Saluda Mountain on September 12, 1937. Photograph by W.H. Thrall. Collection of Frank Ardrey.

chief engineer for the railroad. Miraculously, the threat of revoking the charter was all that was needed to initiate a spurt of construction, and the tracks joined with the Western North Carolina in 1886 at Asheville Junction in the small community of Best, North Carolina, known today as Biltmore.

Originally, the Asheville & Spartanburg Railroad consisted of track laid in 5' broad gauge. By the late 1880s the line had been converted to standard gauge.

In 1881 the line came under the management of the Richmond & Danville Railroad. During the 1880s the Asheville & Spartanburg Railroad operated somewhat autonomously from the Richmond & Danville and boasted a roster of five locomotives, three passenger cars, two combination mail/baggage cars, and a single revenue car.

The Saluda section of track was well known to railroaders for its dangerous and often deadly grade. When Coleman and Pearson decided upon the 4.7% grade, both agreed it would tax crews to

their absolute limit. It was not long after the tracks reached the town of Saluda in 1878 that the first fatalities occurred. In 1880, 14 men died on Saluda, and other deaths quickly followed. In 1886 nine more died; in 1890 three died; and in 1893 another three lost their lives.

It was not until three successive wrecks occured in 1903 that Southern Railway was prompted to consider abandoning or developing new operation procedures. An engineer, W. P. Pitt Ballew, was involved in the first of the three wrecks, and he survived to be largely credited with developing a new operation policy which drastically reduced the risks.

With Southern locomotive #440, Ballew had departed the Asheville yard with 11 cars of coal and two general merchandise cars. As the train crested the mountain, Ballew applied the brakes and realized from the faint hiss that he had lost his brake pressure. At the same time, the conductor in the caboose at the end of the train noticed the pressure gauge was pegged on zero. Ballew blew his whistle to have the brakemen, who were riding on the roof-

Two Southern 4-4-0 Americans pull a four-car train up Saluda Mountain on a postcard titled "In the Land of the Sky, N.C." The Southern Railway would later employ its largest locomotives to handle the traffic on Saluda, including 2-8-8-2 articulateds and 2-10-2 Santa Fe types. Collection of Doug Walker.

Number 4052, an Ls-2 class 2-8-8-2, storms up Saluda on September 14, 1938. Photograph by W.H. Thrall. Collection of Frank Ardrey.

Southern Railway Ps-2 class #1341 moves up Saluda Mountain during September 1938. Engine #5028 serves as a pusher on train #27. Photograph by W.H. Thrall. Collection of Frank Ardrey.

walks, tie up the hand brakes.

After determining the train was a runaway, Ballew yelled to the crew to jump and save their lives. The engineer and fireman jumped and hurtled down a cinder-covered embankment. The conductor, realizing the train was lost, decided to separate the caboose from the train by pulling the coupling pin. While the conductor started pulling the pin, a brakeman who had been on the roof-walk jumped to the roof of the caboose. As his feet landed safely on the caboose, the conductor separated the hack from the train. The conductor and brakeman were then able to apply the hand brake on the caboose, slow it to a halt, and begin calmly recomposing themselves. They heard the wreck a few moments later as the train crashed at the bottom of the mountain.

The train of 13 cars was a total loss. Only the caboose with the conductor and brakeman survived. The train crew found Engineer Ballew near death at the bottom of the enbankment and in need of extensive medical attention.

While Ballew recuperated, two additional wrecks claimed two more lives. By 1903, 27 men had died in freight accidents, but fortunately, no fatalities had occurred involving a passenger train.

While recovering in an Asheville hospital, Ballew put much thought into how operations on Saluda Mountain could be made safer. He developed a plan for safety tracks to be installed along the steepest part of the grade. Runaway trains would be brought under control by switching them onto safety tracks, which ran uphill. By having the safety track constructed upgrade, gravity and the crews could bring the train under control. The first track was to be installed one mile south from the top of Saluda, above Sand Cut, and the second was to be installed at the foot of Saluda, near the community of Melrose.

Ballew summoned the local superintendent, G. R. Loyall, to his bedside and explained the idea. Loyall was so impressed with the proposal that he ordered the safety tracks installed. The two tracks were in service before the end of the year. The first track was 1,080 feet in length and was built on a grade which varied from 4.3 to 9.9%. Logs and dirt were piled at the end of the first safety track to bring to a halt any train not brought under control

Engine #4526, a Ms 2-8-2, pauses at Melrose, North Carolina, the base of Saluda Mountain, during September 1937. Photograph by W.H. Thrall. Collection of Frank Ardrey.

Engine #5045 serves as the helper ahead of road engine #5023. The date is September 16, 1948. Photograph by Frank Ardrey.

Ls-2 class 2-8-8-2 #4056 is photographed at safety track #1 on Saluda Mountain on September 3, 1937. Photograph by W.H. Thrall. Collection of Frank Ardrey.

by gravity alone. The second safety track was longer—1,464 feet. The grade was generally steeper and ranged from 5.47 to 10.3%.

The railroad manned the switches on the turnouts to the safety tracks 24 hours a day. The switch was always aligned to the safety track until the engineer of a descending train blew a special "Saluda" whistle of a long, short, and long blast. This was a signal that the train was under control, and the switchtender would align the switch to the main line.

Today, the switchmen are gone due to the installation of an electronic timing block. If an engineer keeps his train to eight miles per hour or slower, the track is realigned from the safety track to the main line.

Saluda has not recorded a fatality since September 25, 1940, when an Ls-2 2-8-8-2, #4052, ran away and was diverted up safety track #1. Engineer "Turk" Pope gave instructions for the crew to jump while the train was still well above the safety track, and all but the fireman obeyed the command. The fireman froze at his post and rode the train down the mountain. He died when the engine traveled the length of the safety track and crashed into the piles of dirt and timber at the end. His death was caused

The Southern Railway experimented with additional traction to help with pusher duties on the Saluda grade. Baldwin designed this "experimental tractor" in 1917 to achieve the hoped for effect. The experiment was not a total success. It was soon discovered much of the traction gained by the extra set of drivers was lost when the coal and water supplies were depleted on the tender. After a few short years the gear under the tender was replaced by traditional tender trucks and the 2-8-0 gear was used to construct a traditional Consolidation locomotive. Courtesy of the Pennsylvania Railroad Museum.

by the forward shifting of the coal from the tender when the locomotive struck the obstacles at the end of the track. The coal pinned the fireman to the fire-

Train #9 heads up Saluda Mountain on September 5, 1937, with 2-8-0 #4544 in the lead and #5021, a 2-10-2, serving as the pusher. Photograph by W.H. Thrall. Collection of Frank Ardrey.

This photograph depicts the efforts to retrieve the #4052. This accident in 1940 resulted in the last fatality to occur on Saluda Mountain. Courtesy of the North Carolina State Archives.

door, and he subsequently died from the weight.

Diesels have not escaped the treachery of Saluda. On September 20, 1964, six F-7s were damaged when a runaway roared down the mountain. The crew realized very quickly that a runaway situation had developed, and all abandoned the train except for a flagman and the conductor, who rode out the wreck in the caboose. The men wrapped mattresses around themselves and were thus protected. The wreck resulted in 23 destroyed cars of coal and $69,500 in damage to the six F-7s. The train crew found five of the six units still under power when they reached the crash site at Melrose.

Knoxville Route

Another route into and out of Asheville follows the French Broad River and is often referred to as the Knoxville Route. It connects with the Southern Railway lines in East Tennessee. The line travels northwestward through Marshall and Hot Springs, North Carolina, and into Tennessee through New-

port. All the while the route follows one of the easiest paths known to railroad construction—along a meandering river, in this case the French Broad. This particular route eliminated the need for tunnel construction or steep grades.

The route along the river had long been used by the inhabitants of Buncombe and Madison counties. It was along the French Broad River that a drover's route was established to provide a means for farmers and traders to transport their products to market. Large flocks of turkeys and herds of cattle were often seen being herded along the trail. This in turn promoted additional enterprises along the route in the form of inns, taverns, and livery stations after stagecoach service was introduced.

After the railroad was constructed, Hot Springs, North Carolina, became a popular tourist stop. Naturally warm springs in the area were believed to possess medicinal properties, and tourists bathed in the springs to alleviate certain ailments. The hot springs were developed, including the construction of a large inn to accommodate the bathers. With the increased passenger traffic, the railroad constructed a large station to handle the overflow of tourists.

Most visitors were willing railroad travelers who came to see the natural springs; however, the railroad did have passengers who did not travel on their own accord. Hot Springs, North Carolina, is also known for the German prisoner-of-war camp which was operated in the community during World War I. Many of the locals, not having much contact with the outside world, were astonished to hear

On October 18, 1951, steam locomotive #1455, a 4-8-2, crashed into another train, led by diesel unit #4216. The two photographs illustrate the damage to both the diesel and the steam locomotive. The wreck occurred at Craggy, North Carolina. Photograph by Shelby Lowe.

The passenger station at Hot Springs, North Carolina, was an exceptionally busy place when tourists stopped in to visit the natural springs in the area. Collection of Bruce Sprinkle.

Passenger train #4, led by FP-7 #6133, rolls past Newton, North Carolina. The #6133 is preserved today at the North Carolina Transportation Museum in Spencer, North Carolina. Photograph by Frank Clodfelter. Courtesy of UNC-Asheville.

German. After the armistice was signed, the railroad transported the POWs to ports for the long trip home.

The French Broad route is best known for a passenger train the Southern Railway marketed under the name Carolina Special. The train originated in Cincinnati, Ohio, and traveled to Spartanburg, South Carolina. The line traveled through Knoxville and Newport, Tennessee, through Hot Springs and Marshall in Madison County, North Carolina, through Asheville, and down Saluda Mountain to Spartanburg.

With the time involved in the careful descent of Saluda Mountain, the Carolina Special earned an unflattering nickname, the Carolina Creeper. Nevertheless, the train provided a popular means of travel between Knoxville and Spartanburg. Many World War II soldiers rode the Carolina Special during troop movements and remembered the leisurely pace of the train.

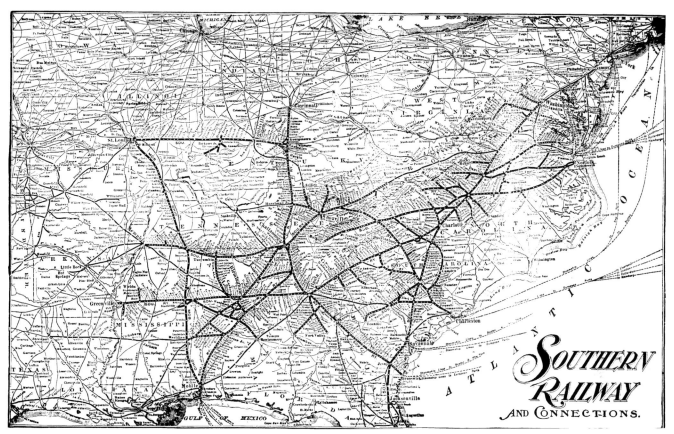

The 1924 *The Official Railway Guide* map of the Southern Railway.

In "Southern" green, units #4198, 4379, 4378, and 4199 pull a mixed freight on February 18, 1958. In 1957 the Southern Railway ceased using the nose herald, and the green paint passed away as well during March 1958. Photograph by Dale Roberts.

Number 1485, a Ts-1 4-8-2, approaches Murphy Junction on train #28. The date is September 15, 1938. Photograph by W.H. Thrall. Collection of Frank Ardrey.

The Murphy Branch

One of the four routes into and out of Asheville acquired the nickname of the Murphy Branch. This particular line originated in Asheville on the Western North Carolina Railroad and was to reach westward to Ducktown, Tennessee. The line, however, only made it as far as Murphy, North Carolina, a distance of 124 miles from Asheville.

In December 1881 the line to Paint Rock, Tennessee, was completed, thus allowing men, materials, and capital to be focused on the completion of the line to Ducktown. By February 1882 the line reached the community of Pigeon River, later renamed Canton, for a total distance of 22 miles of track. It was at Canton that the Champion Paper Company was established in 1906. The line continued to press westward, and grading reached Waynesville in September 1883 for a total mileage of 29 miles from Asheville.

Advance crews were grading for the roadbed to Murphy, and construction crews reached the Cowee Tunnel location (near present-day Dillsboro) by April 1, 1883. On June 1, 1883, the bores on the Cowee Tunnel met and allowed the crews to continue their march westward toward the community of Charleston, later renamed Bryson City.

Much of the labor provided to the Western North Carolina Railroad was in the form of convict labor, similar to the arrangements made between the railroads and North Carolina on the Asheville to Salisbury section and the Saluda section between Asheville and Spartanburg. While constructing the Cowee Tunnel, an incident occurred which is still discussed and has become a part of local myth and legend.

After putting in a day's labor helping to blow rock from out of the tunnel, 19 convicts, a trustee, and a guard were loaded onto a barge to be ferried from the work site to the labor camp. Due to seasonal flooding, the Tuckasegee River was swollen with rain runoff. The barge overturned, drowning the 19 convicts, who were shackled together. The trustee, who was not shackled, saved the life of the prison guard. Most witnesses believed the trustee would be freed for his heroism, but this was far from the case. Upon the guard's revival, he noticed his wallet and $30 missing. Upon searching the trustee,

The marketing department of Southern Railway promoted the cool mountains of Western North Carolina as the "Land of the Sky" in its marketing brochures. Courtesy of *The Official Railway Guide.*

the wallet and cash were recovered, prompting the return of the trustee to shackles.

Locals often refer to the deaths of the convicts and firmly believe the tunnel and surrounding area is haunted by the ghosts of the 19 men. By most accounts, the men were buried on the hill through which the tunnel is drilled.

Construction pressed on, and by December 1885 the rails had progressed 78 miles west of Asheville to Jarret, a community on the Nantahala River. On April 30, 1886, the line under construction and the remainder of the projected route came under control of the Richmond & Danville Railroad. The line was then referred to as the Western North Carolina Division of the Richmond & Danville Railroad.

Poors Manual announced on June 1, 1886, that the line was being converted from 5' broad gauge to a standard gauge of 4' 9". In April 1891 the line was within two miles of Murphy and intended to connect with the Marietta & North Georgia Railroad within the next few weeks. Rain and subsequent flooding delayed the proposed connection for three months while washed out sections of track on the newly constructed sections near Tomatla, as well as older sections close to Asheville, were repaired. The connection had to wait until July to be completed. A total of 124 miles of track—track which wound around river bends, ran through tunnels, rode over grades

of 4.6%, and scaled mountains 3,500 feet in elevation—had taken nine years to construct.

To celebrate the arrival into Murphy, the Western North Carolina Railroad decided to hold a barbeque for the men who had constructed the line. The locals, however, decided to crash the picnic, and a large brawl subsequently erupted. The railroad men were able to save themselves from the melee by boarding a train and steaming out of Murphy.

Of the four routes into and out of Asheville, the Murphy Branch carried the least traffic. In 1886 the average train was only four to five cars in length. However, in 1916 the line proved invaluable when severe flooding struck Western North Carolina.

Within 24 hours, reports record, 25 to 30 inches of rain fell on the area as the result of a meteorological phenomenon. A hurricane entered the Gulf of

Southern Railway F-7 #6718, originally built for the AGS in November 1950, b/n 12355, pulls a string of empty log cars westbound on the Murphy Branch. The locomotive was retired in 1973. Courtesy of Ramsey Library, UNC-Asheville.

Ks-1 class #695 coasts light downhill near Topton, North Carolina, on May 23, 1947. Photograph by R.D. Sharpless. Collection of Frank Ardrey.

An early wood-burning locomotive on the Western North Carolina Railroad is photographed at Halls Station, North Carolina, in 1887. Courtesy of Western Carolina University.

With the floodwaters of July 1916 rising so quickly, some crews were forced to abandon their locomotives while still under steam. Photograph by William Barnhill. Collection of Cary F. Poole.

This Southern Railway yard photograph shows the flooded passenger area and boxcars stranded by the high water. Courtesy of the Barnhill Collection, Pack Memorial Library, Asheville, North Carolina.

The debris left as the floodwaters begin to recede. Courtesy of the Barnhill Collection, Pack Memorial Library, Asheville, North Carolina.

Washed out section of Southern Railway track in Western North Carolina. Note the man on the tracks over the washout. Courtesy of the Barnhill Collection, Mars Hill College, North Carolina.

Southern Railway 2-8-0 #874 rests amid the debris after floodwaters have receded. The Asheville roundhouse is in the background. Courtesy of the Barnhill Collection, Pack Memorial Library, Asheville, North Carolina.

Retrieval efforts to remove lumber and debris wedged under the railroad bridge in Asheville, North Carolina. Much of the lumber was salvaged, thus reducing losses due to the flood. Courtesy of the North Carolina Collection of Pack Memorial Library, Asheville, North Carolina.

The Asheville, North Carolina, yard on September 13, 1966. A GP-9, originally numbered 303 for the Live Oak Perry & Gulf, then numbered 299, later to be renumbered 6251, leads a string of F-units on a mixed freight. Photograph by J.H. Wade. Collection of Frank Ardrey.

Mexico and moved inland from the Mississippi/ Alabama border, and a second hurricane moved inland from the Carolina coast. The two fronts collided and stalled over Western North Carolina, leaving much of the area under several feet of floodwater.

Of the four Asheville routes, the Murphy Branch was the only line to escape large-scale destruction. The Asheville to Knoxville route, the Asheville to Salisbury route, and the Asheville to Spartanburg route were either largely destroyed or out of service. The tracks suffered horrible damage, including 77 complete washouts between Statesville and Ridgecrest. The city of Asheville was devastated by the flood, and the inhabitants found themselves with only one entry for relief supplies, rebuilding materials, and transportation out of the area.

Relief supplies had to be transported from Atlanta, Georgia, on the Western & Atlanta Railroad to Marietta, Georgia. There the supplies were transferred to the Marietta & North Georgia Railroad and transported through the communities of Canton, Elijay, Blue Ridge, and Mineral Bluff before finally arriving at Murphy. At Murphy, the supplies were transferred to the Southern Railway for transport on the 124-mile trip to Asheville.

Although the route into Asheville from Marietta was largely single-tracked, it was estimated that a train passed any given point every 30 minutes. After nine months of ferrying supplies into the city of Asheville, the other three lines were finally rebuilt. The Murphy Branch itself was in deplorable shape due to the heavy tonnage it had carried over the previous nine months.

The four routes into and out of Asheville made that city an extremely important rail center. To have two railroads compete against each other for the honor of being the first to reach the city illustrates how important the city was perceived by investors, merchants, and developers.

Once the four routes had become established, traffic grew steadily from local manufacturers, logging/timber concerns, and mining. The importance of Asheville was further established when traffic which had originated in many other parts of the country passed through the city.

In the single month of November 1926, the Asheville classification yard handled 54,722 cars. In a typical month, the terminal handled the service needs of 2,252 locomotives, 1,875 for freight and 377 passenger. Another 250 locomotives were serviced outside the Asheville terminal but fell under the jurisdiction of that terminal. The handling of this increased traffic resulted in a new engine facility consisting of a 25-stall roundhouse, 106 feet deep in the stalls, complete with a 100-foot turntable.

During World War II, acute shortages of materials occurred, causing the restriction of lumber. To provide a solution to this critical problem, a sawmill

The Southern Railway Passenger station in Asheville, North Carolina, as it appeared on a postcard postmarked 1906. Collection of Jim King.

An As-11 class 0-8-0 switcher at work in the Asheville yard in the early 1940s. The former car shed can be seen in the upper left-hand corner, and the coaling tower in the upper right-hand corner of the photograph. Courtesy of the Highlands Research Center, Ramsey Library, UNC-Asheville.

Ks-2 class 2-8-0 Consolidation #711 serves as pusher at the foot of Red Marble Mountain near Nantahalah, North Carolina. Courtesy of Ramsey Library, UNC-Asheville.

A day on the Murphy Branch. Southern Railway Ps-2 #1256 was photographed near Willets, North Carolina, on August 23, 1947. Train #17 consisted of a mail/express car and a single passenger coach. Estimated speed, 30 mph. Photograph by David W. Salter.

As train #17 struggles up the 5% grade near Topton, North Carolina, the speed has dropped to approximately 10 mph. Photograph by David W. Salter.

After cresting the grade at Topton, the tracks open into a broad valley between Andrews and Rhodo, North Carolina. Estimated speed is 35 mph. Photograph by David W. Salter.

Transition from steam to diesel. A diesel and a steam locomotive await their assignments at the sand tower in the Asheville, North Carolina, yard. Courtesy of UNC-Asheville.

A steam locomotive is being turned on the Asheville, North Carolina, turntable in 1940. Courtesy of the Austin-Brooks Collection, Ramsey Library, UNC-Asheville.

was constructed on Southern Railway property to convert scrap material into usable lumber. After the mill went on line in 1943, it was projected that 850,000 board feet of lumber could be processed each year.

Much of the processed lumber ended up on bridges

The Asheville shops once carried out extensive re-building on steam locomotives. Circa 1940. Courtesy of the Austin-Brooks Collection, Ramsey Library, UNC-Asheville.

or piers, both of which suffered tremendously from the increased war traffic. After the conclusion of the war, the mill continued to turn out lumber for the railroad. As of 1993, the mill is seldom used but completely capable of being reactivated at a moment's notice.

In 1951 additional work was initiated to help modernize the Asheville yard. The railroad hoped to salvage the old yard office building but needed to relocate the structure a third of a mile away. The salvage was completed by jacking the three-story building onto a flatcar and towing the flatcar and

Number 4058, an Ls-2 class 2-8-8-2, is being turned on the Asheville turntable. This particular locomotive was purchased new from Baldwin in 1928 and served until 1951, when it was retired. Courtesy of Pack Memorial Library, Asheville, North Carolina.

This photograph depicts the scrapping of a 2-8-0 Consolidation in the Asheville, North Carolina, yard. Courtesy of the North Carolina Archives.

The Asheville shop in 1949 as the hostelers and shop crews prepare the steam locomotives for their daily assignments. Photograph by E.L. Griffin. Collection of Jim King.

Ex-Southern Railway locomotive #1251, a 4-6-2, is used as a stationary boiler in Swannanoa, North Carolina. The photograph was taken on April 19, 1947, by J.H. Bruner. Collection of Mike O'Neil.

Southern Railway #865 was one of the 2-8-0 Consolidation Class Ks, which were common in Western North Carolina for freight work. The locomotive was purchased new from Baldwin in 1906 and retired in August 1953. It was photographed in Hickory, North Carolina, by Tom Reese.

structure to its new foundation using a steam locomotive, #1874. At the new location, the building was slid from the flatcar onto its new foundation.

The refurbishing costs for the yard exceeded $600,000 but greatly aided the speed of classifying cars in the Asheville facility. The most noticeable improvement was the lengthening of the tracks to accommodate blocks of 150 cars or more. By classifying cars in blocks, switching duties were greatly reduced. The yard was rebuilt to include 13 tracks to handle

classifying duties. Six of the tracks were assigned to handle inbound or outbound traffic which would travel east (to and from Salisbury) and south (to and from Spartanburg). Three tracks were assigned to handle trains to or from Knoxville, and four tracks were designated for classifying local traffic to such points westward as Canton and Murphy, North Carolina, and northward to Bulls Gap, Tennessee.

Not only was Asheville an important rail center as far as operations were concerned, the region surrounding the city also produced one native son president of the railroad, Harold Hall, and became the retirement community for a second president, Dennis William Brosnan.

Harold Hall was a product of Western North Carolina, a man who was born in Nantahala but who claimed Andrews as his hometown. Hall had hoped to study engineering at the University of Tennessee but enlisted in the Navy when he came of age during World War II. While waiting for acceptance into gunnery school, Hall was taught telegraphy by his father, a Southern Railway employee. In this manner, he held a temporary job with the Southern Railway until he was called up by the Navy.

Upon his return from World War II, Hall fully in-

In July 1953, the Asheville coaling tower was dynamited. The Southern Railroad had dieselized and the facility was no longer needed. Note the spectators who have sought refuge behind a tank car to observe the demolition. Photograph by E.L. Griffin. Collection of Jim King.

An "extra," led by engines #4197, 4377, and 4196, is photographed on September 8, 1955. Photograph by Dale Roberts.

A K class 2-8-0 Consolidation, #776 sits at rest in Asheville. Many of the K class locomotives were later rebuilt to Ks-1 or Ks-2 classes. Collection of Tom L. Sink.

Number 599, a 2-8-0 Consolidation, pulls a mixed freight in Asheville, North Carolina. Collection of Tom L. Sink.

An A-B-B-B-A lash-up is photographed on Easter Sunday, 1957. Engines #4180, 4364, 4360, 4361, and 4181 pull across the Glendale Avenue Crossing one mile east of Biltmore, North Carolina. Photograph by Dale Roberts.

A freight train passes the Biltmore, North Carolina, depot on October 10, 1956. The power consists of engines #4188, 4369, 4368, and 4189. Photograph by Dale Roberts.

A young boy watches engines #4144, 6169, and 6119, an A-B-A set, pull past the Biltmore, North Carolina, depot on July 24, 1955. Photograph by Dale Roberts.

tended to pursue his dream of a degree in engineering. After persistent calls to fill in temporarily as an agent-telegrapher at Bryson City, however, Hall never looked back. His first promotion occurred at the age of 21, when he was appointed train dispatcher out of Asheville.

Hall continued to rise steadily by being appointed trainmaster on the New Orleans & Northeastern and, later, superintendent of the Birmingham, Alabama, division of Southern Railway in 1961. Later in the same year, he was appointed by Dennis William "Bill" Brosnan as superintendent of the Southern's Asheville division. This came as a complete shock, since Hall would be supervising many of his former bosses.

Harold Hall's climb up the corporate structure continued when he was appointed vice president under Graham Claytor in 1970. This placed Hall into the inner circle of a five-man management committee which governed the Southern Railway. In 1976 he was appointed executive vice president, and this appointment clearly moved Hall into the role of heir apparent as president of the railroad.

In 1979 Hall succeeded Stanley Crane as president, a position he retained until 1982, when the Southern Railway merged with the Norfolk & Western Railroad to form the Norfolk Southern Corporation.

In the early 1980s, the Southern Railway found itself competing with the newly created megarailroad, the CSX Corporation. Hoping to avoid being squeezed by the new corporation, Hall entertained the idea of a merger with the Norfolk & Western Railroad. The financial facts supporting the merger were overwhelming. CSX would operate 24,000 miles of track, and the proposed merger between the Southern and Norfolk & Western would operate 17,600 miles of track. However, while managing less track mileage, revenues and profits were always the bottom line. CSX had revenues of $4.5 billion, and the proposed merger between the Southern and Norfolk & Western was projected to generate revenues of $3.2 billion. Net profit, however, was listed as $218 million for CSX verses $413 million for the newly created corporation of Norfolk Southern.

Thus, Harold Hall of Andrews, North Carolina,

SD-35 #3055 is photographed at Oyama Yard, Hickory, North Carolina. The date is March 1974, and the photograph is by J.H. Wade. Collection of Frank Ardrey.

served as the last president of the Southern Railway. He later served as a vice president for the newly created Norfolk Southern Corporation.

Upon his recent death, Norfolk Southern recognized his contributions and organized a funeral train to bring his body home to Andrews from Norfolk, Virginia. The modern locomotives, clad in black bunting, pulled the funeral train through portions of the old Southern territory. The last row of seats in a coach had been removed so that a platform could be installed to allow viewing of the casket as the train made its way to Andrews. Many railroad employees paid their last respects by standing at attention as the body of the last president of the Southern Railway made its way through the Old Fort Loops, through Asheville, and out to the Murphy Branch and its final destination of Andrews.

The rise of one of Hall's predecessors had been just as spectacular. Unlike Hall, however, D. W. "Bill" Brosnan had the benefit of a college education—a degree in civil engineering from the Georgia Institute of Technology.

Bill Brosnan was a far different person from his later counterpart. Most observers would agree Brosnan was a mechanical genius, but he lacked interpersonal skills. Brosnan never shied away from a legal fight, even if it meant appealing to the U.S. Supreme Court. He often insisted on a court battle because he sincerely believed, "We're going to win, and we'll win because we're right."

Brosnan maintained a summer retreat at Almond, North Carolina, which quickly became interwoven with local folklore. The retreat became host for an annual meeting of the vice presidents, superintendents, and other various officials, which Brosnan conducted in a camp revival atmosphere. The participants of the meeting often arrived full of trepidation because Brosnan used the meetings to publicly promote, demote, and dismiss members of the railroad's management.

Members of the management were called forth by Brosnan, completely unaware of their impending fate. Upon walking to the front, the summoned party's achievements or shortcomings were shared by Brosnan with the assembled members of the management. Brosnan would then heap praise on those to be promoted or offer a public condemnation on those to be demoted.

The #4137 rolls by on Thanksgiving Day, 1947. The lead unit, an F-3, is shown in the "E-6" paint scheme of 1947-1948. The cables unit is a phase-2 F-3B in the same paint scheme. Photograph by Dale Roberts.

For the management member who suffered the worst fate, dismissal, the ultimate insult was yet to come. Brosnan rationalized that a dismissed employee was no longer gainfully employed by the railroad; therefore, the railroad was not obligated to transport the individual out of Almond. And it must be noted that the railroad was the only transportation into or out of the retreat compound.

While Bill Brosnan was known as a tough taskmaster, by simply adapting to new schedules he often could save the railroad hundreds of thousands of dollars on the purchasing of new locomotives. By utilizing current locomotives to their maximum level of effiency, purchasing of new locomotives was curtailed.

Brosnan had a natural ability to adopt new ideas for the Southern Railway which were currently under research on other railroads. He deliberately did not have the Southern Railway at the forefront of research and design, but he was very quick to implement a proven design after it had been field-tested elsewhere. He reduced operating costs, trimmed unprofitable lines, and reduced personnel costs during his tenure as president from 1962 until 1967. All of his savings helped establish the Southern Railway as

An E-8, #6907 emerges from Jarretts Tunnel on its trip from Asheville to Salisbury, North Carolina. Photograph by Frank Clodfelter. Courtesy of UNC-Asheville.

Engine #4248 leads units 4412, 4413, and 4249 on a snowy January 19, 1955. Engine #4248 was involved in a crossing accident four years later when it hit a tanker truck. The locomotive was totally destroyed in the ensuing fire. Photograph by Dale Roberts.

On a very cold day with heavy snow falling, engine #6119 leads 4138 and 6714 while pulling a passenger train. The date is February 15, 1958. Photograph by Dale Roberts.

one of the most profitable regional railroads in the country.

While diplomacy was not his strong point, Brosnan helped make the Southern Railway a viable, money-making corporation which served the region with pride. A personal marketing strategy promoted by Brosnan helps to illustrate his methods. A slogan printed on plaques, pens, pencils, and note pads read "It Can't Be Done"; however, the *'t* was crossed out, thus implying "It Can Be Done."

Brosnan presided over a lean and trim company which earned money for its stockholders and investors and provided an adequate career for those who could take the heat.

While Almond, North Carolina, played an important role for the annual meetings, Asheville later became Bill Brosnan's retirement home. Upon his death, Brosnan was buried at Calvary Episcopal Church, south of Asheville. On his gravestone is inscribed the customary birth and death dates, as well as the simple inscription, "He Was a Railroading Man."

As of 1995, when this volume goes to press, the four routes into and out of Asheville are still in operation. The Asheville yard still handles 800 to 1,000 cars a day, though a far cry from 50,000 a month during the peak of activity in the 1920s. At one time, the Asheville yard employed 350 employees—in 1993, only 35.

The Asheville to Salisbury route carries trains on a daily basis. Coal traffic bound for the Catawba Elec-

E-8 #6903 and FP-7 #6141 are photographed at the Asheville, North Carolina, roundhouse on August 8, 1975. Photograph by Frank Clodfelter. Courtesy of UNC-Asheville.

tric Plant often employs mid-unit helper locomotives to move the long drags of coal hoppers through the Old Fort Loops.

The Asheville & Spartanburg line is still in operation, but rumors point to a possible elimination of traffic on this historic section of track. Norfolk Southern hopes to abandon the line and consolidate the traffic on other existing lines. The high costs of operating on Saluda are often cited as the largest single reason to abandon the line.

The French Broad River route to Knoxville carries a large portion of the traffic which rolls through Asheville. Coal loads originating in Southwest Virginia travel along the French Broad River on their way to eventual destinations in the piedmont area of the Carolinas.

The Murphy Branch, the fourth route into and out of Asheville, has undergone the most noticeable change over its history. Starting in 1982, the L&N Railroad abandoned its section from Blue Ridge, Georgia, to Murphy. This relegated the Murphy Branch to a true branchline status. In 1987 the Nor-

folk Southern Corporation announced its intention to abandon the line from Dillsboro to Murphy, a distance of 67 miles. The rails were to be pulled, but literally hours before the salvage efforts were to begin, North Carolina purchased the entire section for a bid price of $650,000.

The trackage rights were leased to the Great Smoky Mountain Railroad, which began operations on September 15, 1988, with the intent to haul both freight and excursions. The Great Smoky Mountain Railroad agreed to lease the track for $40,000 a year for 25 years.

From its inception in 1988 until 1993, the excursion business has been extremely popular with tourists. The line travels through some of the most scenic countryside in America, including following for some length the Tuckaseegee and Nantahala rivers and crossing over Lake Fontana.

As many as 200,000 passengers have traveled over the 67 miles of track in a given year. The passengers are pulled behind first generation GP-7 and GP-9 diesel locomotives, as well as #1702, an oil-fired

A Ts-1 class, 4-8-2 #1479 is pulling a passenger train across the French Broad River and is about to approach Murphy Junction. The date is September 14, 1938. Photograph by W.H. Thrall. Collection of Frank Ardrey.

2-8-0 Consolidation steam locomotive. With a fleet of four diesels and one steam locomotive, the Great Smoky Mountain Railroad is poised to handle the increasing popularity of excursions and rising freight traffic.

The Great Smoky Mountain Railroad is negotiating—as of 1994—to acquire the portion of the line from Waynesville to Sylva. This proposed acquisition would not only add 15+ miles to the current 67 miles of track, more importantly, it would also allow the railroad to pull excusions over Balsam Gap. This gap is site of the depot with the highest elevation east of the Rocky Mountains. Projected arrangements point to the Norfolk Southern Corporation selling the track to North Carolina, which would then lease it to the Great Smoky Mountain Railroad under an arrange-ment similar to that of the original line.

Traffic between Canton and Asheville generally generates three trains a day to and from the Champion Paper Company. Additional traffic is generated by the Vulcan Materials Company in Enka, where ballast and crushed stone materials are shipped out by the railroad.

Western North Carolina fully illustrates the cyclic nature of railroading. The area was served initially by short line railroads, which, due to many reasons, were soon absorbed by larger railroads. These rail-roads became divisions of even larger railroads—until the cycle reached its peak, and unprofitable lines were then cast off to be picked up by short line operators, as with the Murphy Branch.

Balsam, North Carolina, circa 1960. The station was the highest depot in elevation east of the Rocky Mountain. The station was later moved to the opposite side of the tracks and survives today as a bed and breakfast inn. The Balsam Inn, as shown in the background, has recently been restored to its for-mer grandeur and is open for business as an inn. Collection of Jim King.

The Canton train is being double-headed by locomotives 630 and 573. The Champion Paper Company, located in Canton, North Carolina, represented one of the largest shippers on the entire Southern Railway System. Collection of Tom L. Sink.

Double-heading into Canton, North Carolina, on November 5, 1938. The location is the Owl Roost Bridge, just outside the Canton city limits. The train is led by Ks-1 class 2-8-0 Consolidation #630. Photograph by Norman Williams.

Norfolk Southern Corporation locomotive #5136, a GP38-2 built in February 1974, switches cars near Lake Junaluska, North Carolina. The photograph was taken in December 1987 by Kent S. Roberts.

Southern Railway Locomotive Classes

Wheel Configuration	Class	Name
0-4-4T	A	Forney
0-6-0	A	Switcher
0-8-0	A	Switcher
2-6-0	D	Mogul
2-8-0	G, H, I, J, K	Consolidation
2-8-2	M	Mikado
2-10-2	S	Santa Fe
4-4-0	B	American
4-4-2	C	Atlantic
4-6-0	E, F	Ten-Wheeler
4-6-2	P	Pacific
4-8-2	T	Mountain
2-6-8-0	L	Articulated
2-8-8-2	L	Articulated
4-4-4-4	n/a	Four-truck Shay

An upper case letter represented the class of locomotive, while a lower case "s" represented a superheated locomotive.

TALLULAH FALLS RAILWAY

Few railroads embodied the soul of mountain railroading as did the Tallulah Falls Railway. The railroad, which ran from Cornelia, Georgia, north to Franklin, North Carolina, was seldom out of debt but was much beloved by the country folk it served.

In 58 miles of track, the line traversed 54 trestles and many sections of elevated roadbed. The entire length of the line was contained within the two Georgia counties of Habersham and Rabun and the North Carolina county of Macon. Most of the residents of the three counties it served referred to the Tallulah Falls Railway as the "Old TF."

The official start of the railroad is listed as January 27, 1854, when the Georgia General Assembly passed a bill authorizing the construction of a rail line to extend from Athens to Clayton. The name chosen for the endeavor was the Northeastern Railroad, and it was chartered in 1856. However, actual grading and construction were postponed until 1871. While construction was proceeding from north of Cornelia, the line was sold to the Richmond & Danville Railroad. During this ownership, the railroad projected eventual construction northward to Clayton, Georgia.

The Blue Ridge & Atlantic Railroad acquired the line in 1883, but five years later the railroad entered into its first of many receiverships. The receivership ended in 1897, when the railroad was incorporated as the Tallulah Falls Railway Company.

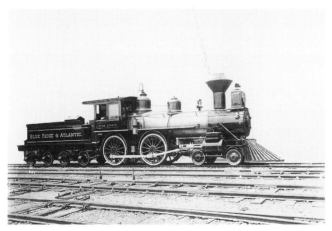

Blue Ridge & Atlantic locomotive #1 was a 4-4-0 American constructed by the Baldwin Locomotive Company. The Blue Ridge & Atlantic Railroad was a predecessor to the Tullulah Falls Railroad. Courtesy of the Railroad Museum of Pennsylvania.

In 1904 the connection was made to Clayton, and in rapid order the line reached the North Carolina state line in 1905. At this approximate time, the Southern Railway acquired the capital stock of the railroad. Macon County, North Carolina, voted on and passed a bond issue to fund the construction of the line into Franklin, North Carolina. The first train arrived in Franklin in June 1907.

The year after reaching Franklin, the railroad entered into a one-year receivership, emerging from that receivership only to enter receivership again in 1923. The line never emerged from court-ordered receivership until its demise in 1961.

In 1933 the Interstate Commerce Commission

United States Railroad Administration
W. G. McADOO, Director General of Railroads
TALLULAH FALLS RAILROAD
TIME TABLE NO. 17
Effective Sunday, Oct. 20th, 1918, 6:00 A. M., Eastern Time.

SOUTHBOUND			Eastern Standard Time	NORTH BOUND		
5 2d class Tuesday Thu. Sat.	**11** 1st class Daily	Mi	STATIONS.	**12** 1st class Daily	**6** 2d class Monday wed. Fri	Capacity of Track in Cars
A. M.	P. M.		Lv. Ar.	P. M.	P. M.	
8 00	2 10	58	........Franklin........	1 55	3 30	71
8 40	s 2 23	53	........Prentiss........	s 1 39	3 00	19
9 05	s 2 38	48	........Otto........	s 1 24	2 38	23
....	f 2 50	43	....Orlando, N. C.....	f 1 10		
9 40	s 2 56	42	......Dillard, Ga......	s 1 05	1 50	17
9 45	s 3 00	41	......Rabun Gap......	s 1 00	1 35	52
10 05	s 3 09	38	....Mountain City....	s 12 50	1 15	16
10 30	s 3 19	35	........Clayton........	s 12 20	12 55	28
....	f 3 24	33	........Bethel........	f 12 10		
10 50	s 3 29	32	........Tiger........	s 12 12	12 12	17
10 10	s 3 43	28	........Wiley........	s 12 00	11 40	9
10 20	s 3 48	27	........Lakemont........	s 11 54	11 35	8
11 48	f 3 52	25	........Joy........	f 11 48	11 25	19
12 15	s 4 06	21	......Tallulah Falls......	s 11 36	11 00	21
12 20	s 4 11	20	......Tallulah Lodge......	s 11 31	10 45	18
....	f 4 16	19	....Tallulah Park....	f 11 28		3
12 40	s 4 26	16	......Turnerville......	s 11 19	10 20	15
12 55	s 4 34	13	....Hollywood....	s 11 10	10 00	8
....	f 4 39	11	........Anandale........	f 11 04		4
....	f 4 44	9	....Hills....	f 10 59		5
1 30	4 52	8	......Clarksville........	s 10 56	9 33	42
....	f 4 56	6	......Habersham........	f 10 48		5
1 50	s 5 03	5	......Demorest........	s 10 44	8 30	25
2 25	5 18	0	........Cornelia........	10 30	8 00	126
A.M. **5**	P. M. **11**		Ar. Lv.	A. M. **12**	A. M **6**	

All Northbound trains have right of track over trains of same class in opposite direction.
S—Regular stop. F—Stops only when flagged.
Riverside M. P. 50, Norton M. P. 45, York M. P. 40, Parkers M P 34 1-2 Bovard M. P. 30, Burton Jct., M. P. 28 1-2 not shown on Time Card, are Flag stops for trains 11 and 12
Nos. 5 and 6 do not carry passengers.
11 12 stops 20 minutes at Clayton for dinner.   D W. NEWELL, Supt.

The United States Railroad Administration listed four trains a day in 1918 running from Franklin, North Carolina, and Cornelia, Georgia. Courtesy of *The Official Railway Guide*.

Locomotive #75 was a Baldwin-built 2-8-0 Consolidation. The tender carried the name *Rabun Gap Route*. The engine was constructed in 1912. Courtesy of the Railroad Museum of Pennsylvania.

TALLULAH FALLS RAILWAY.

Fairfax Harrison, President, Washington, D.C.			R. L. Butt, Gen. Fht. Agt., Atlanta, Ga.		
F. S. Wynn. Vice-Prest., "			Jno. S. King, Freight Claim Agent, Atlanta, Ga.		
D. S. Abernethy, V.-Prest., "					
E. H. Kemper, Comptroller, "			E. C. Gatewood, Exec. Gen. Agt., Rectortown, Va.		
G. E. Mauldin, Sec'y, "					
E. F. Parham, Treasurer, "			V. A. Slaughter, Live Stock Claim Agent, Washington, D.C.		
J. M. Forney, Auditor, Danville, Va.					
M. F. Hawkshaw, Accountant, Cornelia, Ga.			Geo. H. Dugan, Eng'r Maint. of Way, Washington, D.C.		
W. R. Colklesser, Pur. Agent, Washington, D.C.			D. W. Newell, Supt., Cornelia, Ga.		

No. 4	No. 2	Miles	May 28, 1922.	No. 3	No. 1	....
*5 50 P M	*10 40 A M	0	lve...**Cornelia** δ ..arr.	9 20 A M	5 25 P M	....
4 03 »	10 54 »	4.4	+..... Demorest ..... δ	9 06 »	5 15 »	....
– –	10 58 »	6.0	......Habersham......	– –	5 07 »	....
4 12 »	11 07 »	7.3	+....Clarksville....δ	8 56 »	5 02 »	....
4 16 »	11 11 »	8.9	.........Hills.........	8 49 »	4 56 »	....
4 21 »	11 17 »	10.7	........Anandale........	8 44 »	4 51 »	
4 27 »	11 25 »	13.0	+....Hollywood....δ	8 39 »	4 46 »	
4 37 »	11 34 »	16.1	+....Turnerville....δ	8 29 »	4 37 »	STANDARD—Eastern time.
4 46 »	11 43 »	18.5	....Tallulah Park....	8 22 »	4 26 »	
4 50 »	11 47 »	19.8	... Tallulah Lodge ...	8 19 »	4 22 »	
4 56 »	11 52 A M	20.9	+..Tallulah Falls..δ	8 16 »	4 17 »	
5 10 »	12 04 P M	25.3	..........Joy..........	8 04 »	4 04 »	
5 15 »	12 10 »	26.3	+.....Lakemont.....δ	8 01 »	3 59 »	
5 20 »	12 15 »	27.9	+.......Wiley.......δ	7 57 »	3 54 »	
5 32 »	12 28 »	31.4	+.......Tiger.......δ	7 47 »	3 43 »	
– –	12 32 »	32.7	.......Bethel........	– –	3 39 »	
5 43 »	11 00 »	34.7	+........Clayton.......δ	7 37 »	3 33 »	
5 53 »	1 10 »	37.8	+..Mountain City..δ	7 27 »	3 22 »	
6 01 »	1 18 »	40.5	+... Rabun Gap ...δ	7 16 »	3 13 »	
6 05 »	1 23 »	41.6	+....Dillard, Ga....δ	7 12 »	3 09 »	....
– –	1 29 »	43.8	.....Orlando, N.C.....	– –	3 01 »	....
6 20 »	1 43 »	48.5	+........Otto........δ	6 55 »	2 49 »	....
6 33 »	1 55 »	52.8	+.....Prentiss.....δ	6 43 »	2 35 »	....
6 50 P M	2 10 P M	57.2	arr. +**Franklin** δ .lve.	*6 30 A M	*2 20 P M	....

Trains marked * run daily.   + Coupon stations ;   δ Telegraph stations.

The Tallulah Falls Railway listed four trains a day running the length of its 58-mile line between Cornelia, Georgia, and Franklin, North Carolina, in 1922. Courtesy of *The Official Railway Guide.*

heard petitions to abandon the line, and eventually granted permission to close and sell off the assetts. The decision to close the line was done despite the vehement protests of the local residents served by the railroad. Action to abandon the line was not taken until 1961, and in the meantime, the locals continued to hope the line would emerge from the receivership and once again become profitable.

For a small mountain short line, the Tallulah Falls

utilized a variety of motive power to connect the many mountain communities. The original locomotives were wood-burning 4-4-0s in the classic "American" Whyte wheel configuration. Later steam engines were of the 4-6-0 and 2-8-0 wheel configurations.

A passenger schedule connected the communities of the three serviced counties until 1946. At that time, a grade crossing accident destroyed the sole remaining coach. Outside of Cornelia a truck struck engine #73, causing only $100 worth of damage to the locomotive. The coach, however, was destroyed, and several passengers were showered with glass in the collision.

The Tallulah Falls Railway also operated a "Doodlebug" for a brief period. The short tenure was due to the propensity of the railcar for jumping the tracks. The car still exists (as of 1992) as a private residence outside of Clayton.

In 1948 the Tallulah Falls entered into its third and final round of motive power. With the sale of all but one of the coal-fired steam engines, the railroad purchased two 70-ton switchers built by General Electric. These two locomotives served the railroad until its abandonment in 1961.

Every short line railroad has its share of railroad mishaps and wrecks which become forever part of that line's folklore. The Tallulah Falls had two spectacular wrecks which were talked about by the local mountain folk for many years.

Tallulah Falls "doodlebug" #201 shown north of Clayton, Georgia, on July 25, 1953. Photograph by R.D. Sharpless. Collection of Frank Ardrey.

The #78 pulls across a trestle into Clayton, Georgia, on November 2, 1946. Photograph by R.D. Sharpless. Collection of Frank Ardrey.

The #78 pulls into Clayton, Georgia, as it makes its way across the largest wooden trestle on the line on November 2, 1946. Photograph by R.D. Sharpless. Collection of Frank Ardrey.

General Electric-built #502 is shown crossing a trestle in North Carolina. Courtesy of the North Carolina State Archives.

A Georgia Power Company 0-4-0T narrow gauge locomotive prepares to push two side-dump cars as fill is removed for the construction of the Tallulah Gorge Dam. The photograph was taken March 13, 1924. Collection of Jim King.

The first major accident occurred when a train pulling a children's excursion suffered a derailment. The locomotive and baggage car toppled from the tracks in the accident. The baggage car simply fell over on its side, but the locomotive rolled down the elevated roadbed until its wheels were pointed to the sky. The engineer was crushed to death, and the fireman was severely scalded by escaping steam. The four coaches remained on the tracks with no injuries to any of the children.

The second major accident occurred in 1898 at the Panther Creek trestle. Over 100 feet high, it was the highest trestle on the entire line. When the passenger train was crossing over the highest section of the trestle, the middle supports collapsed. The collapse caused the locomotive, the tender, and the first car to pitch to the bottom of the ravine. Miraculously, the last coach remained on the still-erect portion of the bridge. The coach came to rest mere inches from falling over the side of the trestle and landing on top of the first coach and the locomotive. This accident also had one fatality—a gentleman passenger remembered by the locals as having the last name Ivy.

Since the railroad spent much of its corporate history in receivership, the crews tried to prevent any anticipated legal problems. One such attempt to avert legal responsibility was to pay for the death of any livestock killed by locomotives on the railroad. The railroad preferred paying $75 per animal in order to avoid being taken to court. The crews assisted the railroad by keeping an ample supply of throwing ammunition, in the form of rocks or chunks of coal, in the cab of the locomotive. Using this, the crews could run off, scare, or drive off any livestock which might be between the rails.

The Southern Railway eventually controlled 51% of the stock of the Tallulah Falls Railway. This left the Southern in a commanding situation as to what would eventually happen to the short line. Walt Disney Productions used the railroad for the on-location shooting of the movie *Andrews Raiders*, starring Fess Parker. Walt Disney, himself, entertained the notion of turning the Tallulah Falls Railway into a scenic railroad. After much discussion, the Southern Railway decided not to promote the idea of a scenic railroad and began to seriously look at closing the line.

The local people served by the Tallulah Falls Railway made one last gallant attempt to save the railroad from the creditors, who proposed selling the assets to a salvage dealer. Most of the debt was in the hands of the Railroad Employees Retirement Board. They held a claim for $300,000 for delinquent taxes. The Rabun Industrial Development Company was utilized as the bidding company by local interests to purchase the assets and keep the railroad running. The group entered a bid for $266,000, although they never had cash on hand of more than $100,000. The bid was for the 54 miles from Franklin, North Carolina, south to Clarkesville, Georgia. The remaining four-mile segment was bid on separately by the Southern Railway for $36,000—for the connection from Clarkesville south to Cornelia.

The Rabun Industrial Development Company offered the Railroad Retirement Board $50,000 to settle its claim of $300,000. The Railroad Retirement Board refused this initial offer. After the railroad assets were liquidated, the board received only $17,000 for its claim of $300,000.

In 1961 and 1962, the tracks were recovered for their scrap value by the Midwest Steel Company.

ASHEVILLE & CRAGGY MOUNT RAILROAD
ASHEVILLE & NORTHERN RAILROAD
ASHEVILLE & SOUTHERN RAILROAD

The Asheville & Craggy Mount Railroad ran north from the city of Asheville and along the French Broad River until the tracks eventually reached Beaver Dam. The line was chartered on July 22, 1890, and was originally to extend from the top of Craggy Mount to the top of Mitchell's Peak.

An amended charter was issued in 1903 which allowed the line to determine the need for an extension across the French Broad River and to extend toward Burnsville in Yancey County or as far toward the Tennessee state line as the company cared to build. All together, however, the railroad built only seven miles of track.

From 1890 to 1892 the line had 2.5 miles of track from Chestnut Street to the then city limits and the Golf Club Station. At that time, the line was operated by steam locomotives, but only during the summer months. The line remained abandoned from 1897 until 1900, when it came under the control of Richard S. Howland. Howland purchased the securities, rebuilt the line, and converted it to electric.

By 1902 an extension was completed to Locust Gap, and this 1.5 mile addition was operated by steam locomotives. On January 1, 1905, the Asheville & Craggy Mount Railroad resumed operations under its own account when Richard S. Howland agreed to relinquish control.

In April of 1906, the Southern Railway acquired control through the purchase of existing stock. Along with this acquisition, the Southern Railway also picked up the interests of the Asheville & Northern Railroad.

The Asheville & Craggy Mount #11, a 0-4-2T, operated in the northwest part of Asheville to a connection with the Southern Railway on the French Broad River. The connection was known as Craggy Station. Courtesy of the Austin-Brooks Collection, Ramsey Library, UNC-Asheville.

The Asheville & Craggy Mountain #1 was a Brill-built electric locomotive. Collection of Marvin Black.

Craggy Station was located on the Southern Railway northwest of Asheville, North Carolina, on the French Broad River. The photograph is from 1904. In 1906 the line was sold to the Southern Railway. Courtesy of the Austin-Brooks Collection, Ramsey Library, UNC-Asheville.

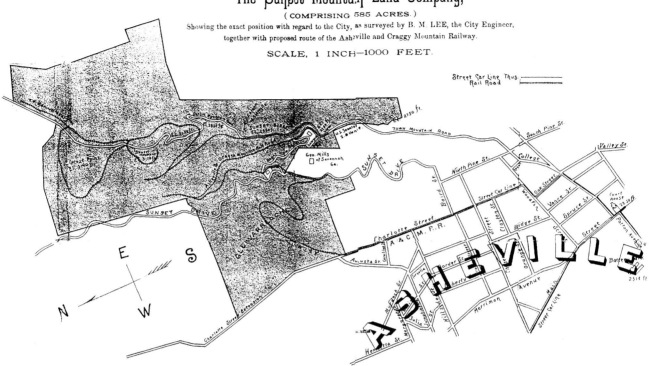

This undated map shows the proposed line of the Asheville & Craggy Mountain Railway and the development on Sunset Mountain. Courtesy of Pack Memorial Library, Asheville, North Carolina.

The Asheville & Northern Railroad was chartered by the state, but track was never laid, nor rolling stock purchased. The holding company simply owned a franchise which allowed the construction of a possible line from Asheville to the Tennessee state line.

The Asheville & Southern Railroad was a line organized by A. B. Andrews and his associates and was to operate solely in Buncombe County, North Carolina. According to the Articles of Association filed with North Carolina, "the line was to make a connection with the Southern Railroad at or near Asheville and extending northward down the French Broad River valley on the east side of the same valley." A second connection was to be made with the Southern Railway across the French Broad River, on its west side, above the mouth of Beaver Dam Creek.

The Asheville & Southern was operated by the Asheville & Craggy Mount Railroad until the parent line's purchase by the Southern Railway in 1906. The total length of the line was approximately five miles. The Asheville & Craggy Mount Railroad was totally absorbed by the Southern Railway in 1926.

Asheville quickly developed a streetcar system, which in time became extensive. The city was reportedly the second city in the South, behind Richmond, Viriginia, to have developed a streetcar system. The system grew until it was the fourth largest system of its kind in the South. The system served not only downtown Asheville and the surrounding areas, but was also constructed north to the town of Weaverville, a distance of six miles.

The list of streetcar companies is lengthy, includ-

The scene above depicts the extent of the flood damage to the car barn in Asheville, North Carolina. The worker is standing on sand deposited by the receding waters. Courtesy of Pack Memorial Library, Asheville, North Carolina.

An Asheville Rapid Transit Company streetcar moves up Horseshoe Curve near Sunset Mountain in Asheville, North Carolina. The Asheville Rapid Transit Company had no other connections, thus losing additional freight and passenger business to other streetcar lines. Collection of Doug Walker.

"Birney" type electric car #6, circa 1910. Trolleys first ran in February 1889 and were replaced with bus service on September 16, 1934. Courtesy of the Austin-Brooks Collection, Ramsey Library, UNC-Asheville.

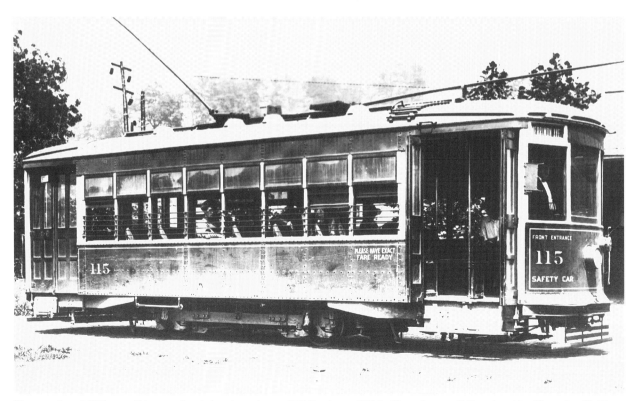

Four-wheel "Birney" type electric street car #115, circa 1910. Courtesy of the Austin-Brooks Collection, Ramsey Library, UNC-Asheville.

ing those which merged, were liquidated, or entered receivership. The list includes the Asheville Street Railroad Co., the Asheville Loop Line Railway, the Asheville Rapid Transit Company, and the Sunset Mountain Railway Company. Besides the lines which were actually constructed, speculation and dreams alone would have added considerably to the list.

One such line which relied on speculation was the completion of the line from Weaverville to Galax, near the Tennessee line, with a connection on the Carolina, Clinchfield & Ohio Railway. The residents of Yancey and Madison counties rejected the proposed bond issue, and the line never materialized. The discussions did go as far as arranging for the Weaverville Power Plant to supply electricity for the project.

Pack Square, Asheville, North Carolina, on September 16, 1934. This was the last day of operations for the trolleys. Operation of electric cars had begun in February 1889. Courtesy of the Austin-Brooks Collection, Ramsey Library, UNC-Asheville.

"CAN'T AND NEVER WILL"
Remembering the Carolina & North-Western
by
ROBERT D. WALKER, JR.

Fifty-eight years ago this past June, a significant railroad event took place in upper Caldwell County, North Carolina. The Carolina & North-Western Railway ran its last passenger train to Edgemont, North Carolina—the end of the line. Freight service continued once a week, and later, as needed, until 1938. After 1938 the line was abandoned from Valmead, North Carolina (above Lenoir), to Edgemont.

That is the end of a story that had its beginning around 1884, when railroad fever hit Lenoir, North Carolina, located in Caldwell County. That year the narrow gauge Chester & Lenoir Railroad struggled into Lenoir with much fanfare.

The Chester & Lenoir Narrow Gauge Railroad had its beginning prior to the Civil War in the form of the broad gauge King's Mountain Railroad. The gauge of this railroad was five feet wide, and it had run from Yorkville to Chester, South Carolina, in the 1850s. It was completely wrecked during the Civil War and was not restored afterward.

The King's Mountain Railroad lay abandoned some seven years after the war. Then a new company was chartered to take over the abandoned roadbed. Two companies were involved in the procedure. One was located in North Carolina, and the other in South Carolina.

The two companies were the Carolina Railroad in North Carolina, chartered February 8, 1872, and the Chester & Lenoir Narrow Gauge Railroad, chartered in South Carolina on February 26, 1873. Some grading was done on both roads for a few months. A common goal was reached when the two railroads legally merged on April 3, 1874. Grading resumed after the 1874 merger, and with the use of convict labor the line reached York, South Carolina, in March 1875. By June 1876 the track reached Gastonia, North Carolina. Construction began a slowdown, and track did not reach Lincolnton, North Carolina, until July

On June 2, 1884, the first train arrived in Lenoir, North Carolina. The Chester & Lenoir #2 was a narrow gauge 0-6-0 locomotive. Collection of Doug Walker.

1881. The railroad then had exhausted its funds and could not build the line to Lenoir as originally planned.

The directors of the Chester & Lenoir Railroad appealed for help from the Charlotte, Columbia & Augusta Railroad. The directors agreed to lease the railroad to the Charlotte, Columbia & Augusta in return for completion of the railroad into Lenoir, a distance of some 37 miles. Before the lease could take effect, on September 22, 1882, the Charlotte, Columbia & Augusta Railroad was merged into the Richmond & Danville Railroad. The directors of the Richmond & Danville decided to honor the lease of the Chester & Lenoir Railroad, and the construction began almost at once.

On June 2, 1884, the line was completed to Lenoir, North Carolina. The finished railroad consisted of 110 miles of track, which stretched from Lenoir, North Carolina, to Chester, South Carolina. There were six miles of dual gauge track between Hickory and Newton, North Carolina. The railroad had 7 locomotives, 12 passenger cars, 2 business cars, and 111 freight cars.

The Chester & Lenoir Railroad began to haul freight and passengers, and after several years, the line fell into receivership. It was reorganized as the Lenoir & Chester Railroad; however, most still refer to the line as Chester & Lenoir. This reorganization did not help much; and to make matters worse, the Richmond & Danville Railroad went into bankruptcy in 1893. The lease of the Chester & Lenoir Railroad was cancelled that same year. Late in 1893, the Richmond & Danville Railroad was reorganized and was to include the Chester & Lenoir Railroad. Since the Chester & Lenoir was having problems in covering expenses, the line was turned back over to a receiver, who was appointed as administrator to handle lawsuits and unpaid bills.

The receiver managed to operate the line until 1897. At this time, the line was reorganized as the Carolina & North-Western Railway. This organization apparently had the blessing of the Southern Railway, who had merged the Richmond & Danville Railroad into its extensive system of railroads. The

Governor Zebulon B. Vance visits Lenoir, North Carolina. In the background is a Cheraw & Chester coach. This line was also 3' gauge and connected with the Chester & Lenoir Narrow Gauge Railroad in Chester, South Carolina. Collection of Doug Walker.

Carolina & North-Western Railway continued to be a narrow gauge road, but that changed in 1902 when the road was standard gauged.

When the Chester & Lenoir Railroad was reorganized as the Carolina and North-Western in 1897, the railroad was going to be expanded into Watauga County and on to Bristol, Tennessee. The only survey made from Lenoir northward was the Yadkin Valley route. This route was to go north through Indian Grave Gap, down the Yadkin River to the mouth of Buffalo Creek, then on up Buffalo Creek to Cooks Gap, and down to Boone, North Carolina. Later, the survey was to extend to Todd, North Carolina. A connection was to be made with the Virginia-Carolina Railroad (the Virginia "Creeper") at that location. This route would give the Carolina & North-Western a northern connection and would allow coal from the Virginias to head southward on a much shorter railroad route. However, the survey of this route was never finalized, and Lenoir, North Carolina, became the northern terminus of the Carolina & North-Western.

When the Chester & Lenoir Narrow Gauge came to Lenoir in 1884, it "sparked railroad fever." A number of companies offered stock and subscriptions for railroad construction, but none was built. However, a charter was issued in 1891 to the Caldwell Land & Lumber Company for construction of a railroad. No one did anything except boast and talk. Finally, in 1893, a line was constructed from Lenoir to Collettsville, North Carolina. The line was known as the Caldwell & Northern Railway. At completion, the line had two locomotives, one passenger car, and twenty-one flatcars. The Caldwell & Northern, at this time, was more logging railroad than common carrier, for it mainly supplied the lumber mills that supported the numerous furniture factories in and around Lenoir.

The Caldwell & Northern Railway gradually began to extend itself in a southwesterly direction and soon was making money for its owners. By 1903 the Caldwell & Northern had extended the railroad up Wilson Creek when it more or less ran out of money. The Carolina & North-Western Railway gained control of the company in 1905 but operated it as a separate subsidiary. The Caldwell & Northern Railway completed its line up Wilson Creek to Mortimer, North Carolina, where a sawmill was in operation. By January 1906 the Caldwell & Northern Railway was finished to Edgemont.

Railroad expansion fever hit the tiny village of Edgemont, and in July 1908 the Caldwell & Northern Railway issued a proposal to extend beyond Edge-

The W.M. Ritter Lumber Company operated a bandsaw mill at Mortimer, North Carolina. The lumber company had several narrow gauge logging lines which spanned out over Caldwell County. It was at Mortimer that W.M. Ritter connected with the Carolina & North-Western Railway. Collection of Doug Walker.

Crew from W.M. Ritter Lumber Company hand loads sawed lumber from the narrow gauge line to the crew of the Carolina & North-Western, to be reloaded onto standard gauge cars. Collection of Doug Walker.

mont via Coffey's Gap and on to Boone, North Carolina, by the newly proposed Watauga Railroad. This railroad was to extend from Coffey's Gap (Kelsey, North Carolina) to Boone. The Caldwell & Northern Railway would extend its line from Edgemont to Coffey's Gap, a length of 18 miles, if the Watauga Railroad and the Blowing Rock community would pledge $225,000. The money was never raised.

In 1910 the Caldwell & Northern Railway was merged into the Carolina and North-Western Railway, much like the Chester & Lenoir Railroad buyout of 1897. Better service could be provided this way.

Railroad expansion died down, and the Carolina & North-Western settled down to hauling freight and passengers. Finished lumber was coming from the mills of the W. M. Ritter Lumber Company of Columbus, Ohio. Mortimer was a model mill village with electric lights in the houses and lumber plant. By comparison, the typical local home in the area was without electricity and indoor plumbing.

Although railroad expansion had died down, a

number of proposals were made, but none became reality. Among such proposals were an interurban line between Charlotte and Edgemont, and another to run between Edgemont and Pineola, with a connection to the East Tennessee & Western North Carolina Railroad and a possible connection with the Virginia-Carolina Railroad at Todd, North Carolina. This new railroad was to be called the Aery & Northwestern Railroad.

The trains of W. M. Ritter's logging lines continued to haul logs to the mill in Mortimer, but timber was getting farther away from the mill as the cutting increased. One of the lines left Mortimer on the opposite side of the valley from the Carolina & North-Western and went toward Lost Cove Cliffs and then through several switchbacks. The line proceeded around the base of Chestnut Knot and then to Upper Creek, nearly reaching the headwaters of that creek. There, the line went toward the Linville Gorge area and stopped due to the extreme roughness of the terrain.

The mill started running out of timber, and some

Carolina & North-Western #206 as shown in its Baldwin builder's photograph taken in 1913. Courtesy of the Railroad Museum of Pennsylvania.

The Edgemont depot has been preserved long after the tracks have been removed. Today, it serves as a summer home for a local family. Collection of Doug Walker.

The route of the Carolina & North-Western north of Hickory, North Carolina, and the logging operations which interchanged with it. Courtesy of Chris Ford.

workers were laid off. The operation continued with two log camps, but the worst was yet to come.

In June 1916, after two days of hard, steady rain, rivers and creeks began to overflow their banks. As the water rose, it took out various sections of the railroad from Lenoir, thus isolating the lumber towns of Mortimer and Edgemont. Water was so high in the mountains that it began to wash away houses and barns. Eventually the floodwaters reached the W. M. Ritter plant, and it, too, was swept away by the raging water. Much of the cut lumber in the yards was washed away as well. The force of the water caused the brick walls of the power plant to collapse.

When the floodwaters receded, most of Mortimer was gone. What was not gone had been knocked off its foundation and rested downstream. The Carolina & North-Western tracks were gone from Collettsville to Mortimer, and from there to Edgemont. Crews from the Southern Railway and the Carolina & North-Western began rebuilding the track. Crews from W. M. Ritter's plant began to rebuild track down from Edgemont to meet the railway crews. The Ritter crews also began the job of rebuilding their own logging lines.

The flood of 1916 brought many changes to upper Caldwell County. The mill, which was running out of timber before the flood struck, now faced the decision of whether to expand its logging lines or close down the operation. The W. M. Ritter Company chose the latter and, on September 7, 1917, moved its operations from Mortimer, North Carolina, to Freemont, Virginia.

The Ritter operation began to tear down and prepare for shipment all remaining machinery and equipment. Two to three million board feet of sawed lumber had not been destroyed and still remained on the property. After several months, all remaining lumber had been shipped out. The rails were taken up from the various logging lines out of Mortimer, thus exposing the ties. These ties remained embedded in the ground in many areas for the next 50 years.

The Carolina & North-Western Railway was now without a major shipper, but the railroad managed to survive by cutting freight and passenger trains. Several small contract sawmills were still in operation around Roseboro, North Carolina (north of Edgemont), and some logging was done on behalf of the Hutton and Bourbonnais Lumber Company of Hickory, North Carolina. Three standard gauge Shays were operating in and around Edgemont with contract loggers for Hutton and Bourbonnais.

This three-truck Shay, #1, was photographed in 1924 at Edgemont, North Carolina. Speculation is that it is a Hutton, Bourbonnais and Company locomotive. This company was known to have standard gauge lease units in the area after Ritter pulled out. Collection of Doug Walker.

As the hills were being cut, the logging began to slow down. Finally, about 1924 or 1925, logging stopped in the area. At about the same time, Model T Fords were becoming the family mode of transportation. The Carolina & North-Western's passenger business began to fall as a result of the popularity of the automobile. Instead of taking the train, the families now took their automobiles to the mountains for their outings. By 1924 *The Official Railway Guide* listed only one passenger train each way from Lenoir to Edgemont. Still, the people of Edgemont were trying to attract more people to their area. The Edgemont Inn opened and advertised for outings.

Following the Ritter plant closing in Mortimer, the railroad depot closed. Mortimer was in its decline,

Carolina & North-Western #150, a 4-4-0 American, is photographed in Hickory, North Carolina, in March 1941. Collection of Doug Walker.

CAROLINA & NORTH-WESTERN RAILWAY.

Fairfax Harrison, President, Washington, D.C.
F. S. Wynn, Vice-Prest., »
D. S. Abernethy, V.-Prest., »
E. H. Kemper, Comptroller, »
G. E. Mauldin, Sec'y, »
W. R. Colklesser, Pur. Agent, »
Geo. H. Dugan, Eng'r Maint. of Way, Washington, D.C.
L. T. Nichols, Supt., Chester, S.C.
W. A. Corkill, Local Treas., »

W. K. Kearsley, Aud., Chester, S.C.
Major J. H. Marion, Asst. Division Counsel, Chester, S.C.
R. L. Butt, Gen. Fht. Agt., Atlanta, Ga.
Jno. S. King, Fht. Claim Agt., »
E. C. Gatewood, Exec. Gen. Agt., Rectortown, Va.
V. A. Slaughter, Live Stock Claim Agent, Washington, D.C.
E. F. Reid, D. F. & P. A., Gastonia, N.C.

No. 54	No. 2	Mls	April 23, 1922,	No. 55	No. 1		
....	*7 25 A M	0	lv.+**Chester¹** ⦿ ar.	....	6 55 P M	.....	....
....	7 32 »	3	...... Airlee	....	6 26 »	.....	....
....	7 44 »	8	..... Lowry's ... ⦿	....	6 14 »	.....	....
....	7 57 »	14	... McConnells....	....	6 01 »	.....	....
....	8 03 »	16	..... Guthries ... ⦿	....	5 54 »	.....	....
....	8 20 »	23	......**York²**.... ⦿	....	5 36 »	.....	....
....	8 33 »	28	...... Filbert	....	5 26 »	.....	....
....	8 45 »	33	..... Clover ... ⦿	....	5 14 »	.....	....
....	8 54 »	37	...... Bowlin ..	....	5 06 »	.....	....
....	9 00 »	39	.....Crowders.....	....	4 58 »	.....	....
....	9 07 »	42	..South Gastonia..	....	4 50 »	.....	....
....	9 22 »	45	+...**Gastonia³** ⦿	....	4 40 »	.....	....
....	9 35 »	49	..... Dallas ... ⦿	....	4 17 »	.....	....
....	9 49 »	55	..... Hardins	....	4 03 »	.....	....
....	9 53 »	56	... High Shoals ⦿	....	3 57 »	.....	....
....	10 00 »	59	... Long Shoals ..	....	3 51 »	.....	....
....	10 05 »	61	.....Southside	....	3 44 »	.....	....
....	10 10 »	62	.....Laboratory ..	....	3 40 »	.....	....
....	10 16 »	64	+..**Lincolnton⁴** ⦿	....	3 30 »	.....	....
....	10 38 »	73	..... Maiden ... ⦿	....	3 08 »	.....	....
....	10 56 »	80	+...**Newton⁵**... ⦿	....	2 50 »	.....	....
....	11 54 A M	90	+...**Hickory⁶**.. ⦿	....	2 14 »	.....	....
....	12 12 P M	94	....Cliffs......	....	1 57 »	.....	....
....	12 18 »	96	....Rhodhiss.. ⦿	....	1 49 »	.....	....
....	12 25 »	98	..Granite Falls. ⦿	....	1 43 »	.....	....
....	12 33 »	101	.....Saw Mills ...	....	1 35 »	.....	....
....	12 38 »	103	.....Hudson ... ⦿	....	1 29 »	.....	....
....	12 46 »	107	..... Whitnel	....	1 20 »	.....	....
....	12 55 P M	110	ar,..**Lenoir⁷** ⦿ .lv.	....	*1 10 P M	.....	....
†12 50 P M	....	110	lve...Lenoir ,.arr.	9 20 A M	....	.....	....
2 36 »	....	111	....,Valmead	9 10 »	....	.....	....
2 42 »	....	113	.....Warrior	9 02 »	....	.....	....
3 02 »	....	117	..... Olivette.....	8 42 »	....	.....	....
3 12 »	....	118	.....Coffeys ...	8 35 »	....	.....	....
3 25 »	....	120	... Collettsville ..	8 20 »	....	.....	....
3 48 »	....	123	...... Adako ...	8 05 »	....	.....	....
4 10 »	....	127	...... Gorge	7 45 »	....	.....	....
4 40 »	....	131	.....Mortimer... ⦿	7 15 »	....	.....	....
5 00 P M	....	134	ar..**Edgemont** ⦿ lv.	†7 00 A M	....	.....	....

Trains marked * run daily; † daily, except Sunday. + Coupon stations; ⦿ Telegraph stations. STANDARD—*Eastern time.*

CONNECTIONS.

¹ With Southern, Seaboard Air Line and Lancaster & Chester Rys.
², ⁵ and ⁶ With Southern Ry.
³ With Southern Ry. and Piedmont & Northern Ry.
⁴ With Seaboard Air Line Ry.
⁷ With Blowing Rock Stage Line.

The Carolina & North-Western Railway was a booming railroad in 1922. The boom was largely due to large-scale logging taking place around the community of Edgemont, North Carolina. Courtesy of *The Official Railway Guide.*

The #167 was a Baldwin-built 4-6-0 constructed in 1889. The locomotive was acquired second-hand in June 1911 from the Pennsylvania Railroad. Photograph by Tom Reese.

and people were moving away. Those who remained were looking for jobs. After several months, a 10,000-spindle cotton mill was to be located in the town. The mill meant cotton would be shipped in and textiles would be shipped out. Inexpensive power was readily available using Wilson Creek. If this textile mill had been built as planned, it would have provided jobs for about 1,000 workers. This would have contributed immensely to the stabilization of the area's economy, but the hope of getting the large cotton or textile mill proved fruitless. Only a small mill, employing about 100 workers, was actually built. Freight and passenger service dwindled to a single mixed train that went up one day and back down the next. By 1935 the train service was done on an "as needed" basis. Weeds began to grow between the tracks, which became rusty from lack of use.

The Laurel Inn at Mortimer closed in the early 1920s, and the Edgemont Inn closed its doors in the

The #272 doubleheads a freight out of Hickory, North Carolina. The #272 was a 2-8-0 purchased new from Baldwin in 1913. Photograph by Tom Reese.

The #270 leads a doubleheader from Hickory, North Carolina. The lead locomotive was a 2-8-0 purchased new from Baldwin in 1912. Photograph by Tom Reese.

Carolina & North-Western #150, a 4-4-0, is photographed beside a Great Northern Railway boxcar in Hickory in 1941. The #150 was formerly Southern Railway #3850. Photograph by Tom Reese.

Carolina & North-Western #10 has just struck a car at a grade crossing in Hickory, North Carolina, during April 1970. Photograph by Tom L. Sink.

Carolina & North-Western Alco RS-11 is photographed at Peachtree Station in Atlanta, Georgia. The #11 worked for 17 years on the Southern System before being traded to General Electric and resold to the Chicago & Northwestern Railroad. It was the only RS-11 to serve on the Southern Railway System. Photograph by O.W. Kimsey. Collection of Frank Ardrey.

early 1930s. The villages of Mortimer and Edgemont became tiny hamlets in the woods. Mortimer eventually became a ghost town.

Finally, in February of 1937, the Carolina & North-Western Railway petitioned the Interstate Commerce Commission to abandon passenger service between Lenoir and Edgemont. When people heard the announcement, a great crowd showed up at the depot to ride the last train to Edgemont. In June of 1937, the last passenger train was run. Freight service from Lenoir continued for almost another year before it was abandoned in the spring of 1938.

In 1949, when I was a young Boy Scout, I discovered the abandoned depot at Mortimer while on a scouting trip. Some houses were still standing at that time, although they were rotting away. The depot at Mortimer, along with the depot at Collettsville, was torn down in the 1970s. Pieces of the depots were numbered and rebuilt to form a new structure at Frontier Village, an amusement park between Blowing Rock and Boone, North Carolina. When Frontier Village went out of business, the pieced-together depot was moved to the Tweetsie Railroad, where it serves as a museum and theater.

Today, you can drive up Wilson Creek Gorge on the Carolina & North-Western roadbed. Some miles farther up the road are the ruins of the textile mill. There is still among the weeds of the field the remnant of one fire hydrant. The depot at Edgemont has been moved from its original location and is now used as a private summer home. Portions of grades from the Carolina & North-Western, as well as the Ritter logging lines, are everywhere. The general store at Edgemont has remained in its original location for well over 80 years. The store is open only on Fridays and Saturdays during the summer. Various bridge piers remain at Mortimer and Collettsville, reminding us that a railroad was there many years ago. The Edgemont Inn recently burned to the ground. Little else remains of the community.

The line between Hickory and Lenoir, North Carolina, continues to operate as of 1993. As a subsidiary of the Southern Railway, the line hauls general merchandise between Hickory and Lenoir. In the late 1980s, after the merger of the Southern Railway with the Norfolk & Western to form Norfolk Southern, the line was added to the highly successful Thoroughbred Program. In this program, segments of rail line are leased to shortline operators. In this fashion, Norfolk Southern still receives the eventual traffic, but its costs are lowered because the shortline operators have lower overhead operating costs.

The first operator of the line between Hickory and Lenoir was the Commonwealth Railroad of Midlothian, Virginia. This operating company promptly renamed the line the Carolina & Northwestern Railway. Commonwealth operated the line up until May 1993, at which time another shortline operator was to be selected.

Back in the late 1920s and early 1930s, the Carolina & North-Western was given the nickname "Can't and Never Will." The railroad got this nickname because of all the proposals and expansions which never took place. Whether this line continues to operate on a leased basis will determine if the nickname "Can't and Never Will" still holds true.

A single coach and a RPO car are doubleheaded out of Hickory, North Carolina, in 1939 with #270, a 2-8-0, in the lead and #150, a 4-4-0, following. Photograph by Tom Reese.

TRANSYLVANIA RAILROAD

The Transylvania Railroad connected the communities of Hendersonville, Brevard, and Rosman, finally reaching Lake Toxaway.

The original line was named the Hendersonville & Brevard Railroad, Telegraph & Telephone Company. It connected the two namesake communities of Hendersonville and Brevard and was completed in 1894, which relegated it to a rather late status as far as railroad construction was concerned in Western North Carolina.

Ora L. Jones, a noted local historian who compiled a volume entitled *Transylvania County*, believed the railroad to be a major expansion as far as the economic impact on the county was concerned. He wrote, "...with the exception of the old Davidson River Iron Works, Inc., which ceased operations about the close of the Civil War, there were not industrial enterprises of any importance in Transylvania County prior to the coming of the Hendersonville and Brevard Railroad in 1894. Before there were any railroads in other sections of the mountains, Transylvania was as much 'in the swim' as her neighbors, but after the other counties had secured railroad connections with the outside world and the people learned to depend upon this mode of travel, Transylvania became somewhat isolated for a time."

Fleming Ramsuer was the first to survey the line, but the final survey work was completed by Tam C. McNeeley. The railroad operated as an independent line for only five years, at which point it was placed into receivership.

After being placed in receivership, the railroad was purchased by J. F. Hays at auction, and its name was changed to the Transylvania Railroad, with the line being controlled by the Toxaway Company. The sale included all existing materials belonging to the railroad: twenty-two miles of track, all bridges, trestles, and buildings, two locomotives, one first-class

The "Dummy" Laurel Park, Hendersonville, N. C.

The Laurel Park Street Railway was a commuter line which ran from Hendersonville four miles to Laurel Park on Davidson Mountain. The locomotive was a 20-ton Davenport 0-4-0T, built in January 1906, c/n 374. The locomotive originally was built for the McCall Ferry Power Co. in McCall Ferry, Pennsylvania. It later went to the Pennsylvania Water & Power Co. as its #4, then to the Georgia Car & Locomotive Company, a locomotive dealer who used it as a shop engine, #148. From there it was sold to W.A. Smith of Hendersonville, North Carolina. The photograph is from a postcard circa 1911. Collection of Doug Walker.

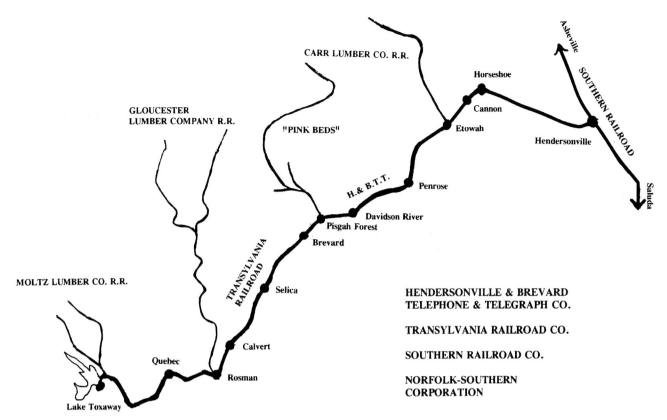

CARR LUMBER CO. R.R.

GLOUCESTER
LUMBER COMPANY R.R.

"PINK BEDS"

H. & B.T.T.

TRANSYLVANIA
RAILROAD

MOLTZ LUMBER CO. R.R.

Asheville

SOUTHERN RAILROAD

Saluda

Horseshoe

Cannon

Etowah

Hendersonville

Penrose

Davidson River

Pisgah Forest

Brevard

Selica

Calvert

Quebec

Rosman

Lake Toxaway

HENDERSONVILLE & BREVARD
TELEPHONE & TELEGRAPH CO.

TRANSYLVANIA RAILROAD CO.

SOUTHERN RAILROAD CO.

NORFOLK-SOUTHERN
CORPORATION

The route of the Transylvania Railroad and the communities it served. Collection of Cary F. Poole.

car, one combination car, three boxcars, one flatcar, two handcars, and miscellaneous supplies and equipment. Hays was elected president of the newly formed company and promptly decided to extend the line an additional ten miles to Rosman. At the time the line was pushed through, in 1900, the community of Rosman was known as Old Toxaway.

Hays launched a petition to support a bond issue in the amount of $25,000. This amount would be used to finance the line to Old Toxaway. The bond issue passed, although it was noted at the time that stiff opposition was said to exist regarding not only the bond issue, but also the construction of the railroad in general. The opposition, naturally, was strongest in portions of the county which would not feel the economic impact of the construction of the railroad.

The line was extended to its longest point at Lake Toxaway in 1903. In this same year, the large inn at Lake Toxaway was completed and the rush by the elite to vacation in Transylvania County had begun.

Under the presidency of J. F. Hays, the Transylvania Railroad established a grand plan to continue

the connection south to Seneca, South Carolina. This route would bypass 35 miles of the existing route owned by the Southern Railway between Asheville, North Carolina, and Seneca.

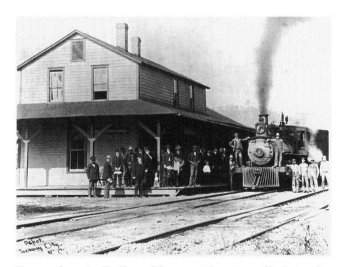

Transylvania Railroad locomotive #2 pulls into the Toxaway City, North Carolina, depot. The community of Toxaway City was later renamed Rosman when the community of Lake Toxaway developed a few miles to the west. Courtesy of Pack Memorial Library, Asheville, North Carolina.

The Southern Railway heavily advertised the Lake Toxaway area and encouraged the development of the area as a tourist haven. Courtesy of Pack Memorial Library, Asheville, North Carolina.

By 1905 six trains a day were passing through Brevard from origins such as St. Louis, New Orleans, Atlanta, and Jacksonville. Dignitaries of the like never seen by the local folk, such as Thomas Edison, Henry Ford, and Diamond Jim Brady, stayed at the inns of Lake Toxaway. With this sort of clientele, the inns were necessarily luxurious. Local townspeople often pointed out with pride that Diamond Jim Brady's private coach was the only car too large to be accommodated by the line in Rosman.

By 1906 the fortunes of the Toxaway Company had begun to fail. The clientele had simply moved to new vacation spots with more luxurious inns, and the Toxaway Company was soon dissolved. The hotel properties were sold to E. H. Jennings of Pittsburgh, Pennsylvania, and the railroad was sold to the Southern Railway. The dreams of a connection to Seneca died with the sale of the Transylvania Railroad, because the Southern already had in place a parallel route.

The #6 was a 4-6-0 photographed in Brevard, North Carolina, in May 1903. The locomotive was originally built by the New York Locomotive Works in 1887. Original photograph by John Allen.

In July 1916 the same massive flood which destroyed three of four Southern Railway routes into Asheville also destroyed the dam at Lake Toxaway. With the destruction of the dam, the lake ceased to exist. The inn closed the same year and was eventually demolished. The dam was not restored until 1960, but by then the tourists could follow the highway to reach the lake.

The inn had boasted of having a very fine sparkling water that bubbled up from the ground near the lake. After the dam collapsed, it was discovered that a freight-car load of scrap metal had been dumped into a hole in the lake bed. From this pile of metal ran a pipe through the dam, and out flowed the "famous" mineral water.

The closing of Lake Toxaway Inn was, in fact, a harbinger of future track cutbacks. The line was reduced to Rosman, and then to Brevard. As of 1994, the current owner, the Norfolk Southern Corporation, has plans of scaling the line back to Pisgah Forest. With the Ecusta Plant located in Pisgah Forest, it is hoped steady freight traffic will prevent any foreseeable track removal.

The Transylvania Railroad benefited by additional revenue from carloads of timber originating from three logging railroads which operated out of the Brevard area. Louis Carr's Carr Lumber Company had a tremendous impact on the economic development of Brevard with both its railroad and lumber business. The Carr line ran in a generally northwestern direction through what is now part of the Pisgah National Forest. In 1912 Carr paid

$1,500,000 for the timber rights to 70,000 acres of land owned by George Vanderbilt.

When Louis Carr agreed to lease the acreage from George Vanderbilt, Carr and Vanderbilt agreed on an expedition to survey the contents of the lease. The trip took ten days to cover the 70,000 acres on horseback. On October 12, 1912, the deal was signed.

In what is now Pisgah National Forest in North Carolina, Carr soon built a sawmill on the site where Vanderbilt had constructed a previous, but smaller, mill. In order to facilitate the hauling of logs to the mill and the shipping of finished lumber to market, the Carr Lumber Company operated some 75 miles of railroad tracks.

Upon George Vanderbilt's death, Mrs. Vanderbilt approached Louis Carr with the offer to sell the 70,000 acres for $5 an acre for a total asking price of $350,000. Louis Carr refused the offer, and the land was instead offered to the U.S. government. That

The logs in the foreground are reportedly two of the largest logs felled by the Gloucester Lumber Company. The men are, left to right, Engineer Jess Galloway, Jason McCall, and Clay Honaker. Courtesy of the U.S. Forest Service.

The crew of a Carr Lumber Company Climax pose beside their locomotive at the Pink Beds, near Pisgah, North Carolina, in 1917. Courtesy of the Austin-Brooks Collection, Ramsey Library, UNC-Asheville.

Log loader #4 of the Gloucester Lumber Company is photographed at Rosman, North Carolina. Welch Galloway is the loader operator. Courtesy of the U.S. Forest Service.

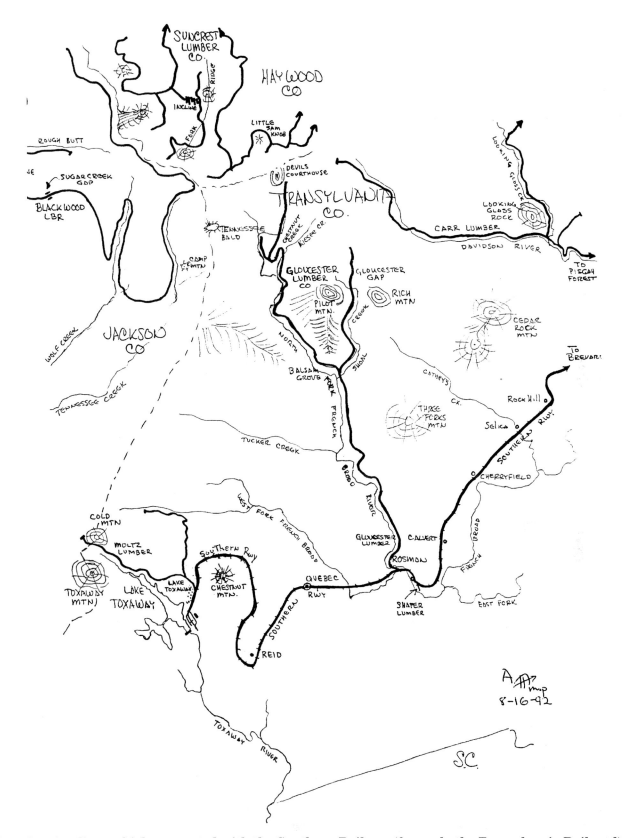

Three logging lines which connected with the Southern Railway (formerly the Transylvania Railroad) are illustrated in the above map. The Moltz Lumber Company Railroad interchanged at Lake Toxaway, the Gloucester Lumber Company Railroad at Rosman, and the Carr Lumber Company Railroad at Pisgah Forest and Etowah, North Carolina. Courtesy of Tom Fitters.

A Shay locomotive belonging to Moltz Lumber Company rests on cribbing while repair work is undertaken. The gentleman on the far right is Carl Moltz, owner and operator of the railroad and lumber mill. Courtesy of the U.S. Forest Service.

The Moltz Lumber Company Shay is pulling a string of loaded log cars to Rosman, North Carolina. Courtesy of the U.S. Forest Service.

The single locomotive for Moltz Lumber Company was a Shay, shown above with a log loader. Courtesy of the U.S. Forest Service.

tract of land is now the Pisgah National Forest.

The Carr Lumber Company continued until 1957, when, bowing to economic necessity, the mill closed. Louis Carr died the next year at age 94.

The Gloucester Lumber Company operated out of Rosman and traveled in a northwesterly direction. One of the leading developers of the local region, Joseph Silverstein, was instrumental in founding the Gloucester Lumber Company in 1911. Silverstein also financed the Toxaway Tanning Company of Rosman, the Rosman Tanning Extract Company, the Transylvania Tanning Company of Brevard, and the

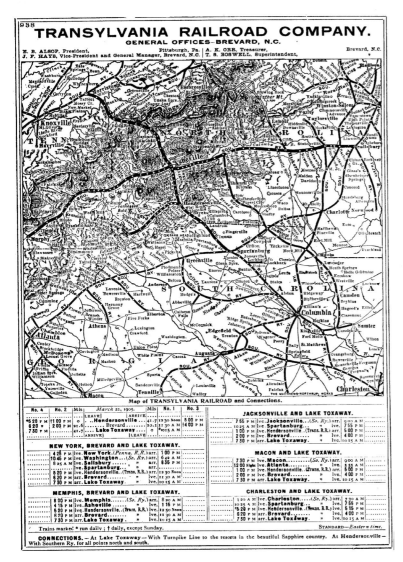

TRANSYLVANIA RAILROAD COMPANY.
GENERAL OFFICES—BREVARD, N.C.

E. B. ALSOP, President,   Pittsburgh, Pa.   A. K. ORR, Treasurer,   Brevard, N.C.
J. F. HAYS, Vice-President and General Manager, Brevard, N.C.   T. S. BOSWELL, Superintendent,

Map of TRANSYLVANIA RAILROAD and Connections.

No. 4	No. 2	Mls	March 22, 1905.	Mls	No. 1	No. 3
			LEAVE		ARRIVE	
*6 20 P M	1 00 P M	0	..Hendersonville...	41.7	12 30 Noon	5 00 P M
6 20 "	2 00 P M	31.6	..Brevard.......	10.3	11 30 A M	4 00 P M
7 30 P M		41.7	...Lake Toxaway...	0	*10 15 A M	
			ARRIVE		LEAVE	

NEW YORK, BREVARD AND LAKE TOXAWAY.

4 25 P M	lve. New York. (Penna. R.R.)	arr.	1 00 P M
10 45 P M	lve. Washington...(So. Ry.)	arr.	6 42 A M
8 25 A M	lve. Salisbury....... "	arr.	8 35 P M
	lve. Spartanburg... "	arr.	
5 20 P M	lve. Hendersonville..(Trans. R.R.)	arr.	12 30 Noon
6 20 P M	arr. Brevard........ "	lve.	11 30 A M
7 30 P M	arr. Lake Toxaway. "	lve.	10 15 A M

MEMPHIS, BREVARD AND LAKE TOXAWAY.

8 00 P M	lve. Memphis....(So. Ry.)	arr.	8 20 A M
4 15 P M	lve. Asheville.... "	arr.	1 16 P M
5 20 P M	lve. Hendersonville..(Trans. R.R.)	lve.	12 50 Noon
6 20 P M	arr. Brevard....... "	lve.	11 30 A M
7 30 P M	arr. Lake Toxaway. "	lve.	10 15 A M

JACKSONVILLE AND LAKE TOXAWAY.

7 55 P M	lve. Jacksonville...(So. Ry.)	arr.	9 00 A M
10 25 A M	lve. Spartanburg.. "	lve.	7 55 P M
1 00 P M	lve. Hendersonville..(Trans. R.R.)	arr.	5 00 P M
2 00 P M	lve. Brevard........ "	lve.	4 00 P M
7 30 P M	arr. Lake Toxaway. "	lve.	10 15 A M

MACON AND LAKE TOXAWAY.

7 30 P M	lve. Macon........(So. Ry.)	arr.	9 00 A M
12 00 Night	lve. Atlanta........ "	lve.	5 55 A M
1 00 P M	lve. Hendersonville..(Trans. R.R.)	arr.	5 00 P M
2 00 P M	lve. Brevard...... "	lve.	4 00 P M
7 30 P M	arr. Lake Toxaway. "	lve.	10 15 A M

CHARLESTON AND LAKE TOXAWAY.

1 20 A M	lve. Charleston....(So. Ry.)	arr.	7 30 A M
10 25 A M	lve. Spartanburg... "	lve.	7 55 P M
*5 20 P M	lve. Hendersonville..(Trans. R.R.)	lve.	5 15 P M
6 20 P M	arr. Brevard........ "	lve.	4 00 P M
7 30 P M	arr. Lake Toxaway. "	lve.	10 15 A M

Trains marked * run daily ; † daily, except Sunday.   STANDARD—Eastern time.

CONNECTIONS.—At Lake Toxaway—With Turnpike Line to the resorts in the beautiful Sapphire country. At Hendersonville—With Southern Ry. for all points north and south.

The Transylvania Railroad made a point of listing in the 1905 *Official Railway Guide* its numerous tourist connections, i.e. New York, Washington, D.C., Jacksonville, Charleston, and other large cities.

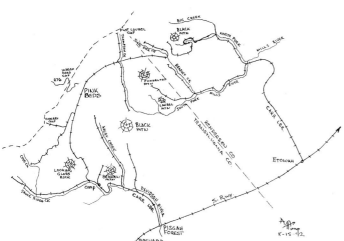

The Carr Lumber Company Railroad had two branches, one which operated out of Pisgah Forest (Davidson River Division), and the other out of Etowah, North Carolina. Most of the land which was logged by the Carr Lumber Company is now the Pisgah National Forest. Courtesy of Tom Fetters.

Southern Railway GP-7 #2187 on the Lake Toxaway line in February 1953. Photograph by R.D. Sharpless. Collection of Frank Ardrey.

Shaeffer Lumber Company of Rosman.

Logging crews of the Gloucester operation could often see crews from the Blackwood Brothers Lumber operation logging on opposing ridges. The Blackwood Brothers operation transported their cut timber through East La Porte and on to Sylva.

The last of the three logging railroads was the Moltz Lumber Company, which operated out of Lake Toxaway and ran in a westerly direction from that community.

The Moltz Lumber Company was incorporated just prior to World War I and operated until the early 1930s. The sole motive power for the logging railroad was one two-truck Shay locomotive. The first rails were laid by black track workers, but later track was laid by local residents. Some sections of the roadbed were so steep as to prohibit the Shay from hauling more than three cars loaded with timber. The general method of operation was for the locomotive to back the empty cars up the track to the loading point and then pull the loaded train forward.

All three logging railroads had but one outlet for their products—the Transylvania Railroad. During the height of the timber removal, the railroad stayed busy hauling two vastly different products: timber from the logging railroads and tourists to the many resorts located in the county.

The Transylvania Railroad could have figured prominently in the development of railroading in Western North Carolina if two connections had materialized. As mentioned earlier, the Transylvania Railroad had its own plan to connect with the Southern Railway at Seneca, South Carolina. In addition, the Tuckasegee & Southeastern Railroad held a charter which would allow it to construct a line from Dillsboro, North Carolina, south to Rosman (Old Toxaway), North Carolina. The line was constructed from Dillsboro to East La Porte, but the connection on to Rosman never materialized. This would have established a direct connection with the Murphy Branch (Western North Carolina Railroad) of the Southern Railway and would have bypassed Asheville, North Carolina, all together.

A more promising proposal went as far as receiving a favorable bond vote from the people of Transylvania County. The Greenville & Knoxville Railroad of Greenville, South Carolina, asked for and received a bond issue to allow it to construct a rail line from Travelers Rest, South Carolina, north into Transylvania County. The Greenville & Knoxville Railroad was to receive $3,000 for each mile of track laid within the county. The tracks were never laid, and as of 1916 the bonds were still waiting for the construction to start.

Today, the Greenville & Knoxville Railroad is the Greenville and Northern Railroad, a short line which survives by switching freight between the two major railroads of CSX Transportation and Norfolk Southern Railroad. The tracks still reach only to Travelers Rest.

CLINCHFIELD RAILROAD

The Clinchfield Railroad was one of the most recent major railroads constructed in the eastern United States. The original idea had been to construct a connecting line from the Ohio River Valley to the Atlantic Ocean. When construction ceased in 1915, a 277-mile line stretched from Elkhorn City, Kentucky, to Spartanburg, South Carolina. This line travels through five states and traverses some of the most picturesque, yet inaccessible areas found in the eastern United States.

Discussions of an Ohio River route to the eastern coast started in the early 1830s, when representatives from North Carolina, Tennessee, Virginia, and Kentucky met at Gate City, Virginia. The meeting originated a plan which would allow for the construction of a railroad to approximate the final route of the Clinchfield Railroad.

With the coming of the Civil War, little more than talk transpired from the meeting held at Gate City. However, a second plan was proposed which called for building a parallel line from Aiken, South Carolina, to Knoxville, Tennessee. This company was organized as the Blue Ridge Railroad, but the Civil War and insufficient financing brought construction to a halt. The resumption of construction was discussed periodically but never carried out, and the idea slowly died.

A group of financiers organized the Charleston, Cincinnati and Chicago Railroad—better known as the Three Cs line—in 1886. The proposal was to extend a rail line from Charleston, South Carolina, to Ashland, Kentucky. This corporation was to become the predecessor to the Clinchfield Railroad. The route would allow the company to tap the rich veins of coal in southwestern Virginia and eastern Kentucky, as well as the iron ore deposits found near Cranberry, North Carolina.

Construction began at Rutherfordton, North Carolina, and quickly progressed south to Camden, South Carolina, by 1888. By 1889 the line had extended an additional 25 miles north, to Marion, North Carolina.

While the Triple C was focusing on construction running north and south of Rutherfordton, work was

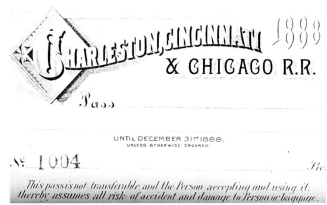

The front of the 1888 pass issued by the Triple-C Railroad. Courtesy of UNC-Asheville.

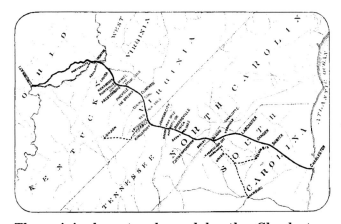

The original route planned by the Charleston, Cincinnati & Chicago Railroad. The map is dated 1888 and printed on the back of a Triple-C pass. Courtesy of UNC-Asheville.

also progressing south from Ashland to Richardson, Kentucky. This construction was initiated through the Triple C's controlling interest in the Chatteroi Railway. The Triple C soon lost its majority interest when the Chatteroi Railway was reorganized as the Ohio & Big Sandy Railroad. The Chesapeake & Ohio Railroad then assumed control of that railway.

In 1890, financial disaster struck the Triple C Railroad. A major investor, Baker Brothers & Company, failed in the financial panic of the time, and court appointed receivership was ordered for the railroad. In May 1893, the Triple C was sold to its bondholders and a new corporation was established: the Ohio River & Charleston Railroad.

By 1898 it was evident that the new railroad would become disjointed and fragmented. Many of the investors wondered if the plan to connect the

Ohio River Valley and the Atlantic Ocean would ever materialize. By August of that year, the line from Marion, North Carolina, to Camden, South Carolina, had been sold to the newly formed Southern Railway Company. The northern line was sold to the Chesapeake & Ohio Railroad two years later, and this left the Ohio River & Charleston only the middle section, which ran south of Johnson City, Tennessee, into the mountains of North Carolina.

In 1902, with new financing secure, the railroad changed its corporate title again to that of the South & Western Railroad. The line pushed south to Altapass, North Carolina, by 1905 and south to Marion, North Carolina, in 1908.

934			SOUTH & WESTERN RAILWAY.			
GEO. L. CARTER, President, Bristol, Va.-Tenn.				MEL H. WEILER, Train Master and Cashier, Johnson City, Tenn.		
J. C. STONE, Treasurer, Bristol, Va.-Tenn.				JOHN A. MUSE, Gen. Fht.& Pas.Agt., Bristol, Va.-Tenn.		
	No. 1	Ms.	*November, 1904.*	Ms.	No. 2	
			(Central time.)			
	†7 20 A M	0	lve.**Johnson City**¹⊙arr.	64.0	3 15 P M	
	7 35 ″	4.9	.........Okolona.....	59.1	2 58 ″	
	7 42 ″	7.3	.......Marbleton.......	56.7	2 51 ″	
	7 46 ″	8.4	.........Taylors.........	55.6	2 47 ″	
	7 53 ″	10.6	..........Unicoi......⊙	53.4	2 40 ″	
	8 01 ″	13.7	.........Fishery.........	50.3	2 30 ″	
	8 08 ″	16.2	...........Erwin.......⊙	47.8	2 23 ″	
	8 18 ″	19.5	..........Chestoa.........	44.5	2 12 ″	
	8 20 ″	20.0	.....Unaka Springs...⊙	44.0	2 10 ″	
	8 47 ″	29.0	........Poplar.......⊙	35.0	1 43 ″	
	8 56 ″	32.0	........Peterson.........	32.0	1 34 ″	
	9 02 ″	34.0	......Huntdale .....⊙	30.0	1 28 ″	
	9 11 ″	37.0	.........Relief.........	27.0	1 19 ″	
	9 23 ″	41.0	....Green Mountain ..⊙	23.0	1 07 P M	
	9 42 ″	47.4	........Toecane......⊙	16.6	12 47 Noon	
	10 10 ″	50.3	......**Boonford**.......⊙	7.7	12 25 ″	
	10 35 A M	64.0	.....**Spruce Pine**...⊙	0	†12 00 Noon	
			[ARRIVE]		[LEAVE]	

The South & Western Railroad, predecessor to the CC&O, listed a simple two-train-a-day schedule in the 1904 *Official Railway Guide*.

In 1901 a battle erupted which could have brewed into a full-blown railroad war. The battle was for the control of the "Breaks" area, which forms a portion of the border of Virginia and Kentucky. George Stevens, president of the Chesapeake & Ohio Railroad, disclosed plans to gain control of the area, which is breached by the Big Sandy River. The river provides a gap known as the "Breaks" in a narrow gorge four miles long with walls towering 1,600 feet in height.

When George Carter heard of the Chesapeake & Ohio's plans to thwart his extension into Elkhorn City, Kentucky, he dispatched Frank Cothran (later president of the Durham & Southern and Piedmont & Northern railroads) to survey the South & Western route. Cothran arrived to find the C&O construction crews grading the roadbed for that railroad's projected route. By word of mouth, the South & Western assembled a crew and began their own roadbed on

the opposite side of the river from the C&O crew.

In a true "Battle of the Breaks"— which was reminiscent of the better known Royal Gorge War, which had been waged 25 years earlier in Colorado—the two crews taunted each other. The South & Western crew occasionally showered the competition with debris from dynamite explosions as they prepared their own roadbed.

The battle was won by the South & Western in court when a judge ruled by "right of prior location" that the railroad could proceed with its route along the Big Sandy River. The ruling went to the South & Western due to the fact that an expedition a few months previous had surveyed the route. An interchange was later established at Elkhorn City, Kentucky, between the Carolina, Clinchfield & Ohio Railway (the successor of the South & Western) and the Chesapeake & Ohio Railroad in 1915.

With the completion of the line to Marion in 1908 and the acquisition of a section of line through a lease of the Lick Creek & Lake Erie Railroad, the S&W finally appeared to be financially secure. The lease with the Lick Creek & Lake Erie provided the South & Western with an extension from Fisk to Dante, Virginia. In this same year, the South & Western acquired a new name, the Carolina, Clinchfield & Ohio, and thus the railroad finally bore the name which is familiar to most people.

With the change of the corporate name, the railroad experienced a tremendous boom in construction. The railroad pushed an additional 60 miles past Marion, through Bostic, and on to Spartanburg, South Carolina. The line was also pushed north to Fisk, Virginia, where it connected with its leased operation, the Lick Creek & Lake Erie Railroad.

In 1908 the railroad had at its disposal 6 steam locomotives, 269 freight cars, and a handful of passenger coaches.

Many people became associated with the fledgling railroad, but one stands tall among all others: George Carter. Carter acquired the remaining assets of the Ohio River & Charleston Railroad in 1902 and was successful in obtaining additional finances for the railroad. He, as a dynamic individual and shrewd businessman, along with the additional capital, pro-

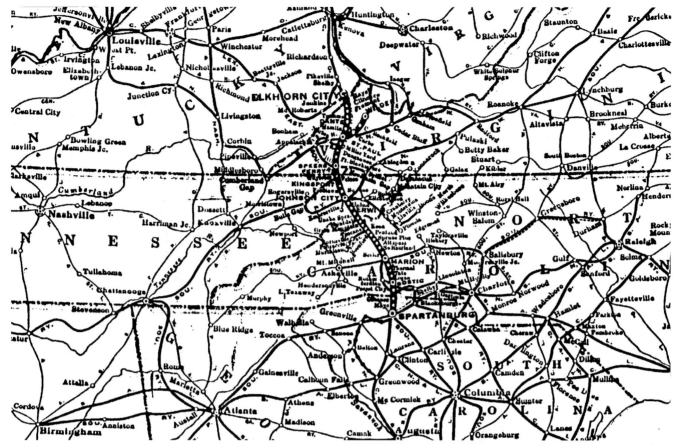

This map illustrates the connections with other various railroads along the route of the Clinchfield. Courtesy of *The Official Railway Guide.*

vided the catalyst for unprecedented growth for the railroad. It was at this time that the railroad's name was changed to the South & Western. Many believe Carter chose the intentionally vague name as a means to confuse the competition. Carter himself was

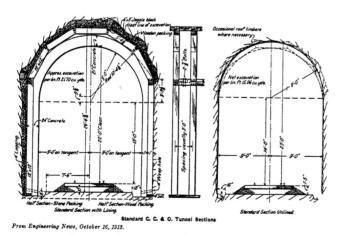

The dimensions of the CC&O tunnels are illustrated above. The tunnels were constructed in such a fashion that no major modifications were needed for the passage of diesel locomotives. Courtesy of *Engineering News.*

a proponent of an Atlantic port terminus for the railroad and believed Southport, North Carolina (south of Wilmington on the Cape Fear Channel), and Charleston, South Carolina, were both port connection possibilities.

His standards for the railroad are evident even into the modern era. An example is the use of steel in all bridge construction. Wood was used only on a temporary basis on bridges until such time as the wood could be replaced by steel. The tunnels were bored to an unheard of standard of 18 feet across and 24 feet high.

Carter's genius was evident by his persuasiveness in keeping financial backers interested in this railroad which had failed several times before.

George Carter had retired as president a few years prior to the completion of the line into Elkhorn City, Kentucky, but he was given the greatest of honors by being allowed to drive home the final spike. At 10:07 a.m. on February 9, 1915, George Carter hammered the last spike in, and the railroad was declared duly open. It had taken 84 years of talk, nearly 50 years of construction, and several corporations, but the bridge route from the Ohio River Valley across the Appalachian Mountains was complete. Much of the credit is due George Carter for his vision, financing, and leadership.

A southbound exits the Vance Tunnel and begins to pull into the Altapass, North Carolina, depot. The photograph was taken from a postcard in the collection of Doug Walker.

When the Carolina, Clinchfield & Ohio Railway was completed, it boasted an impressive list of accomplishments. Many of the achievements regarding construction techniques were viewed as engineering marvels in their day. Since the CC&O was relatively late as railroad construction went, its chief engineers had a chance to observe other railroad construction and adopt techniques to benefit their own needs.

Without benefit of gentle grades along riverbanks, the CC&O crews knew they would have to gradually gain elevation or bore through mountains in order to maintain a relatively level roadbed. The chief engineers proposed a grade of 1.2%, which was well below the accepted standard main line grade of 2%. When the engineers were confronted with a decision to either erect a trestle or bore through the mountain, the construction crews generally chose to bore rather than bridge. Even so, the list of bridges—as well as tunnels—is impressive.

The line contains 51,171 feet of tunnels, or the equivalent of nearly 10 miles of track through mountains. An additional 17,476 feet of track travels over 80 trestles or bridges for a total of 3.33 miles of track.

"The Clinchfield Route" 57?

CAROLINA, CLINCHFIELD AND OHIO RAILWAY
AND
CAROLINA, CLINCHFIELD AND OHIO RAILWAY OF SOUTH CAROLINA

N. S. MELDRUM, President, | 94 Broad Street, New York, Johnson City, Tenn.
G. LEDYARD BLAIR, Vice-President, 94 Broad St., New York,
J. J. CAMPION, Vice-President—Traffic, Johnson City, Tenn.
L. McQUILKIN, Vice-President—Accounting,
L. H. PHETTPLACE, General Manager, Erwin, Tenn.
HORNBLOWER, MILLER & GARRISON, General Counsel, 94 Broad Street, New York,
H. G. MORISON, General Solicitor, Johnson City, Tenn.
O. A. SMITH, General Freight and Passenger Agent,
THEO. DEHON, Gen. Fht. Agt.—Solicitation and Service,

C. W. WALKER, Asst. General Freight Agt., Johnson City, Tenn.
EDWARD C. BAILLY, Secretary, 94 Broad Street, New York,
JOHN W. SANDERS, Treasurer,
CHAS. HEWETT, Assistant Comptroller,
W. A. STARRITT, Purchasing Agent,
L. C. BOY, Industrial Agent,
W. C. HATTAN, Engineer in Charge, Erwin, Tenn.
I. L. McINTYRE, Superintendent,
J. M. FERGUSON, Superintendent of Transportation,
G. F. SHULL, Superintendent Motive Power,

Total Mileage, 309.

MAIN LINE — Stations (partial): Elkhorn City, Bartlick, Haysi, Delano, Clinchco, Fremont, Allen, Nora, Trammel, Dante, Hamilton, St. Paul, Burton's Ford, Carfax, Miller Yard, Dungannon, Hardwood, Wood, Fort Blackmore, Starnes, Hill, Boulder, Speer's Ferry, Kermit, Wayne, Frisco, Rotherwood, Kingsport, Edgewood, Pactolus, Hemlock, Fordtown, Gray, Boone, Indian Ridge, Johnson City, Okolona, Marbleton, Unicoi, Fishery, Chestoa, Lunas Springs, Unet Cove, Poplar, Huntdale, Relief, Green Mountain, Forbes, Toecane, Roses Branch, Bandana, Lunday, Kona, Boonford, Wing, Penland, Spruce Pine, Altapass, Switzerland, Linville Falls, Avery, Pitts, Sevier, Hankins, Marion, Glenwood, Thermal, Tate, Logan, Bostic, Forest City, Harris, Chesnee, Mayo, Enola, Lawson, Spartanburg.

DUMPS CREEK LINE — Wilder, Lednam, Clinchfield Junction, Shaft, Clinchfield Junction, Clinchfield, Carbo.

FREIGHT AND PASSENGER AGENCIES.
Atlanta, Ga.—1223 Healey Building—
 J. E. SCOTT, Commercial Agent.
Augusta, Ga.—302 Lamar Building—
 J. B. SIMPSON, Commercial Agent.
Charlotte, N.C.—913 Johnston Building—
 G. J. MITCHELL, Commercial Agent.
Chicago, Ill.—610 First National Bank Building—
 N. H. HELSTROM, Commercial Agent.
Cincinnati, O.—1101 Union Trust Building—
 F. P. McEWEN, General Western Agent.
 E. S. HINER, Commercial Agent.
Columbus, O.—700 Atlas Building—
 L. E. SAUER, Commercial Agent.
Detroit, Mich.—504 Free Press Building—
 H. O. YANT, Commercial Agent.
Jacksonville, Fla.—102 Graham Building—
 E. F. ELWELL, Florida Agt. & N. B. PARTRIDGE, Commercial Agt.
Johnson City, Tenn.—General Office Building—
 S. C. SMITH, Commercial Agent.
 J. F. LRAKE, Jr., Traffic Service Agent.
Pittsburgh, Pa.—838 Oliver Building—
 E. H. SMITH, Commercial Agent.
Tampa, Fla.—514 Stovall Building—O. Y. ELDER, Commercial Agent.
Valdosta, Ga.—H. K. WILKINSON, Freight Traffic Representative.

CAROLINA, CLINCHFIELD AND OHIO RY. OF SOUTH CAROLINA.
Columbia, S.C.—303 National Loan and Exchange Bank Building—
 J. H. HENDLEY, Commercial Agent.
Spartanburg, S.C.—Andrews-Law Building—
 R. W. HORNSBY, Commercial Agent.

Pullman Parlor-Buffet Car Service
IS OPERATED ON
TRAINS Nos. 37 and 38
Between
SPARTANBURG, S.C.
—AND—
ELKHORN CITY, KY.

A 1924 timetable lists the trains and the mileage between each of the stops on the Carolina, Clinchfield & Ohio Railway. Courtesy of *The Official Railway Guide.*

This Class "B" Shay #693 of the Meadows Company was photographed at Altapass, North Carolina, in 1917. The inscription reads, "Shay—I used this Engine to haul suplys from Altapas on to of Blundy(?) down in the Catawba Valley. Had 2 more Engines for this purpos. It come (?) on 6 switchbacks. 1917. J.H. Harris, Supt. CC&O Ry." Collection of Doug Walker.

North entrance of the Marion, North Carolina, tunnel. This photograph was taken while construction was in process. The year is 1907. Collection of Doug Walker.

A train pulls into Altapass, North Carolina, as it heads north on its scheduled run. The rails reached Altapass in October 1905 and finally reached south to Marion, North Carolina, in September 1908. Collection of Lee Medford.

Forty-three percent of the track is laid on a curve, and the longest straight tangent is only two miles in length (located at M.P. 58-60 and 93-95).

The 1905-1915 construction costs averaged $200,000 per mile, making it one of the costliest railroads to complete. A few short sections were even estimated to have exceeded $1 million per mile. In modern terms, the railroad probably would not be constructed due to the excessive costs. The high costs largely involved the boring of the 55 tunnels, of which the highest concentration is 17 tunnels in 11 miles. This concentration is located south of Altapass, North Carolina, in the area most railroaders refer to as the "Loops."

It is at Altapass that the CC&O reaches its highest elevation above sea level—2,629 feet. The tracks running south of Altapass travel 29 miles through the Loops area to cover an actual distance of only 12 miles. In one particular section of the Loops, a straight line drawn from the south end of the third Washburn tunnel to milepost 208 measures 1.9 miles "as the crow flies." However, it takes the train 16.5 miles of track to cover the same distance. The two small communities of Little Switzerland and Avery, North Carolina, are located in the Loops area. In this particular section of track, a train reverses directions from north to south six times between the two communities.

With the crest in elevation at 2,629 feet above sea level, the two terminus points are at relatively low elevations points. Elkhorn City, Kentucky, is at 795 feet in elevation, and Spartanburg, South Carolina, is at

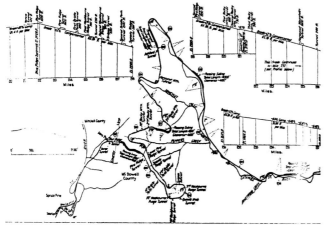

An engineering profile of the Clinchfield Loops illustrates the extreme curves needed to complete this engineering marvel. Courtesy of *Engineering News*, 1909.

765 feet in elevation. Between the two terminus points, however, lies some of the most inaccessible territory in the eastern United States. Not only is much of the track inaccessible due to tunnels and gorges, but also more than 115 of the 277 miles of track are located at 1,500 feet or higher.

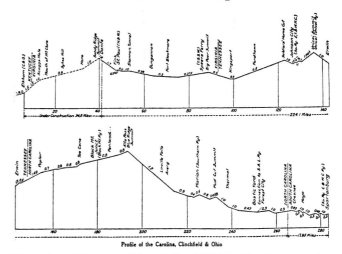

Profile of the Carolina, Clinchfield & Ohio

The elevation profile of the CC&O illustrates the four mountain ranges the line travels through. Ironically, the terminal points of Elkhorn City, Kentucky, and Spartanburg, South Carolina, are only 30 feet apart in elevation—795 feet above sea level for Elkhorn City and 765 feet for Spartanburg. Courtesy of the *Railway Age Gazette*, 1914.

In order to facilitate the construction of the line through the Nolichucky Gorge and the Loops, nine construction camps were established along the roadbed. These camps were occupied by over 4,000 workers, many of whom belonged to ethnic groups never before witnessed by the local mountain people. To provide the cheapest labor possible, recruiters hired laborers in northern cities, and many of the soon-to-be railroad employees were literally straight from the boat and spoke little or no English. Many of the workers recruited were Italians, Germans, Irish, Russians, or Chinese. To supplement the various ethnic groups, many mountain natives and blacks were also employed. The labor camps were truly melting pots in the sense that many different ethnic groups and nationalities were represented.

The camps were often the scenes of riotous behavior. One particular episode sprang from the fact that each laborer was responsible for the cooking of his own meals. Fifteen Italian laborers banded together to hire a fellow countryman to prepare their meals. One day the group returned to find the cook intoxicated and the meal not prepared. The group then pro-

Two small Porter locomotives work south of Altapass, North Carolina, on the Loops in 1907. Photograph by H.H. Carpenter. Collection of C.K. Marsh, Jr.

The CC&O had two cement mixers, one constructed of steel siding and the other of wood siding. The mixers were used to pour the linings of the tunnels along the route. Photograph by H.H. Carpenter. Collection of C.K. Marsh, Jr.

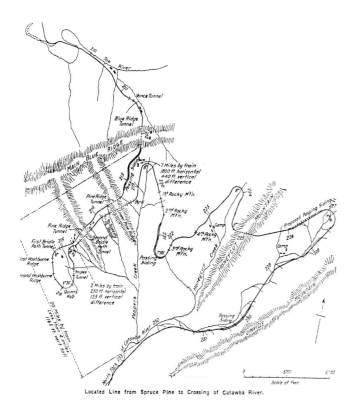

The mileposts of the Clinchfield Loops are clearly labeled as the line snakes down the mountains. The area is only four miles as the crow flies, but twenty miles by rail. Courtesy of *Engineering News*.

ceeded with "Old World" justice. After a trial, the accused was found guilty, tied to a tree, and executed. The Italians were in turn found guilty of murder in Raleigh, North Carolina, and several members of the group spent time in the state penitentiary serving sentences ranging from 5 to 15 years.

Another story told about the unruly behavior demonstrates that even the management of the CC&O railroad was not excluded from the possible violence. The men in a labor camp became restless when the payroll did not arrive, and they proceeded to take matters into their own hands. The camp supervisor heard the commotion, snuck out of the camp, and made his way to the local sheriff's office. With an impromptu posse assembled, the sheriff arrived at the camp to restore order. After an exchange of gunfire, the disturbance was quelled, but not before the discovery of a freshly dug grave. The grave had been intended for the camp supervisor—had the mob found him before his hasty departure.

The Carolina, Clinchfield & Ohio Railway's early history not only chronicles the hardships while building the roadbed, but also records the many legal battles the railroad had to experience. In much the same fashion that the South & Western experienced a legal

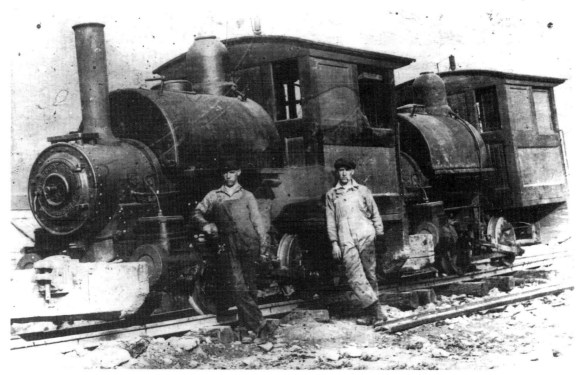

Two narrow gauge 0-4-0 saddle tank locomotives helped with the construction of the tracks leading to Altapass, North Carolina. The locomotives were constructed by the H.K. Porter Locomotive Company of Philadelphia, Pennsylvania. Collection of Lee Medford.

The same flood of July 1916 which destroyed three of the four routes into Asheville, North Carolina, also destroyed portions of the Clinchfield Railroad. A scene from the Loops demonstrates the extent of the damage. Collection of C.K. Marsh, Jr.

battle with the Chesapeake & Ohio for the "Breaks," it and its descendant, the CC&O Railway, had several other legal battles to wage, and three of noteworthy attention were with the Southern Railway.

In 1905 the South & Western entered into a legal battle with the Johnson City & Southern over the possession of a right-of-way. This legal battle in many ways epitomized the railroad's belief that the potential for economic development in Western North Carolina could be accelerated if only one dominant railroad existed for the region.

The Johnson City & Southern, a subsidiary of the Southern Railway, was organized, according to many South & Western supporters, for the sole purpose of driving the fledgling railroad out of business. The Southern Railway was viewed as the dominant railroad in the region, and a line connecting Marion, North Carolina, to Johnson City, Tennessee, would have only strengthened the Southern's grip on the region.

The legal battle over the right-of-way was first heard in the Superior Court of Yancey County, North Carolina, in 1907 and was carried to the North Carolina Supreme Court in the spring of 1908. The right to proceed was awarded to the South & Western.

A second legal fight revolved around the South & Western's desire to establish a crossing with the Southern Railway two miles east of Marion, North Carolina. The Southern Railway refused to grant permission to construct the crossing, and the South & Western went to court to secure permission to tunnel under the Southern's tracks. The Southern Railway, of course, protested the request and countersued to prevent the tunneling. Permission was granted to the South & Western, and tunneling commenced, which allowed that railroad to proceed. As the South & Western was preparing to bore, wooden timbers were put in place to support the Southern's tracks overhead and allow the Southern's operations to continue without any delays or disruption of service. The Southern Railway refers to the crossing today simply as "Clinchcross."

The railroad next hoped to tunnel under the

Southern Railway tracks at Spartanburg, South Carolina, and head to its long anticipated Atlantic terminus. World War I delayed the plan for a few years; then the lease of the line to the Atlantic Coast Line and the Louisville & Nashville railroads in 1925 further stalled the idea. During the Great Depression of the 1930s, the railroad revived the idea and sought and obtained ICC permission but, due to financial concerns, again tabled the plan.

In 1950 the plan was revived once more, but it met with strong opposition by the Southern Railway. Southern, by that time, had achieved a near monopoly on switching duties between the many railroads which entered Spartanburg. After 11 years of commission hearings, court battles, and appeals, approval came in 1962. The Clinchfield lost little time in implementing its plan to bore under the Southern's tracks. Construction commenced immediately, and the tunnel was declared open for business in June of 1963. The project cost the railroad $2 million for an 800-foot-long tunnel. However, the costs were negligible when the Clinchfield was able to interchange directly with the Charleston & Western Railway and the Piedmont & Northern Railroad.

On October 16, 1924, the Carolina, Clinchfield & Ohio Railway entered into a lease with the Atlantic Coast Line and the Louisville & Nashville railroads. The joint lease was to extend for a period of 999 years. Prior to the signing and approval from the appropriate board of directors, a new corporation was formed as an operating company to control the assets of the three railroads which actually comprised the CC&O. Those three railroads were the Carolina, Clinchfield & Ohio; the Carolina, Clinchfield & Ohio of South Carolina; and the Clinchfield & Northern Railway of Kentucky. This new corporation was organized as the Clinchfield Railroad Corporation on December 1, 1924.

The new corporation assumed control of the operations from Spartanburg, South Carolina, to Elkhorn City, Kentucky, on January 1, 1925, as the Clinchfield Railroad. Equipment on the roster of the railroad prior to the formation of the new corporation sported the old reporting marks of CC&O. The new equipment purchased or leased by the Clinchfield Railroad carried the new reporting marks of CRR. At the time of the lease, the Clinchfield carried a roster of 96 steam locomotives and 7,754 freight cars.

The Clinchfield #514 was a Baldwin-built M-2 2-6-6-2 Mallet constructed in 1923. The locomotive had 40" drivers and could deliver 77,400 pounds of tractive effort. This class of locomotive was originally hand-fired through the use of two sets of fire doors. The crews referred to the locomotives as "double door Mallets," and firing on a M-2 was reportedly an extremely exhausting experience. The locomotive was retired on July 30, 1951. Collection of Tom L. Sink.

In 1942 the Clinchfield Railroad instituted one of the most famous and well-received corporate philanthropy programs in the country. In response to the war raging overseas, the Clinchfield Railroad management felt a symbolic gesture needed to be extended to the population of the Appalachians. The management felt a Santa Claus train through the area served by the railroad would not only improve the spirits of the children of the region, it would extend a word of thanks to the shippers on the line. The first Santa train was organized to bring toys and gifts to the children in the impoverished communities along the route.

The route takes the train from Shelbiana, Kentucky, to Kingsport, Tennessee. As the train passes many of the communities along the 120-mile route, candy and small gifts are distributed by Santa and his helpers from the rear vestibule of a coach. In later years, the Kingsport Area Chamber of Commerce has helped to organize the event, collect donated toys, and assist with the massive logistics of the event.

The early Santa Claus trains were pulled by ordinary steam locomotives; then, as first-generation diesels became more common, they took over the hauling responsibilities. Later, the rebuilt Clinchfield #1, a 4-6-0, was used to haul Santa on his annual trip. Early F-units which had been rebuilt were then tapped for the honor. In 1992 a Union Pacific 4-6-6-4 Challenger, similar to a class which served the Clinchfield, was selected to pull the Santa train for its 50th Anniversary. It is estimated 25,000 to 35,000 children line the track in order to see Santa and to receive some of the gifts which are distributed. Upon reaching Kingsport, Santa departs the train to lead the city's annual Christmas parade as the culmination of his trip through Appalachia.

While the Clinchfield Railroad was a major coal hauler, it also provided passenger service over most of its 277-mile route for much of its corporate history. However, on May 2, 1955, the passenger service was discontinued, beginning the demise of a unique community located on the Tennessee and North Carolina state line.

Lost Cove, North Carolina, was a small community located high on the bluff above the Nolichucky Gorge, where it overlooked the Clinchfield Railroad tracks. The only contact with the outside world was via the freight and passenger trains, which brought in necessary supplies and removed cut lumber and acid wood. The passenger service occasionally carried an inhabitant to the outside world and brought in the occasional visitor.

The residents of Lost Cove operated a sawmill, and the Clinchfield Railroad kept a boxcar on a siding below the community. The Covians, as they were called, would lower the cut lumber down a narrow path and load the boxcar with the wood, and the railroad would haul it to its eventual destination. Then the cycle would begin again. Little or no contact was ever established with the Covians on a day-to-day basis.

The settlement was originated just prior to the Civil War by settlers who were either neutral or pro-Union in their loyalty. The settlers had long-standing Republican ideals, thus supporting the belief they were of pro-Unionist persuasion.

Two events signaled the eventual end of Lost Cove. In 1955 passenger service was terminated. The year also marks the death of many of the chestnut stands from a blight. This left little means for the Covians either to make a living or to retain contact with the outside world. A few families held on until 1957, but the new year brought quiet to the near-century-old community.

Sinclair Conley, the longtime schoolmaster for the

community, finally retired in 1957, bringing to a conclusion a unique chapter in education for North Carolina. Conley, who owned a home some 15 miles away at Jacks Creek, Yancey County, commuted in and out of Lost Cove to teach the handful of children. He would hitch a ride out of Lost Cove on a freight train late Friday afternoon, spend a couple of days at home, hitch a ride back to Lost Cove on Monday morning, and commence school that afternoon. Classes were conducted until Friday afternoon, when the cycle would begin again. In 1957, with little hope of road construction to Lost Cove, many of the families began to abandon the settlement. Sinclair Conley etched on a wall of the schoolhouse this epitaph:

Last Sunday School, Nov. 27, 1957

Last Revival, Nov. 1956, Clyde Fisher, Evangelist

School closed forever at Lost Cove, Dec. 17, 1957, Sinclair Conley, 75 years.

Today, the community is solely a ghost town with a few houses still standing. A quick tour of the houses finds an iron skillet still on the woodstove where the original owner left it, a few tattered clothes still hanging in a closet, and little else. Occasionally, a hiker will stop for a rest from walking the steep trail leading from the Nolichucky River below.

The Clinchfield Railroad was constructed to haul coal as inexpensively as possible from the coal fields of eastern Kentucky to the piedmont area of the Carolinas and had several connections with other railroads. On the northern end of the line, the Clinchfield connected with the Chesapeake & Ohio Railroad in Elkhorn City, Kentucky. As the railroad progressed southward, a connection was made with the Interstate Railroad at Miller Yard, located near Norton, Virginia. The Interstate Railroad was also a major coal hauler for the Southwest Virginia region. At both Frisco and Kingsport, Tennessee, the Clinchfield connected with the Southern Railway. Twenty miles farther south, the Clinchfield interchanged once again with the Southern Railway—and with the East Tennessee & Western North Carolina Railroad. The East Tennessee & Western North Carolina remains an independent short line, currently operating under the

An E-3 class, simple articulated 4-6-6-4 #670 thunders through Marion, North Carolina, on April 3, 1947. Collection of David Driscoll.

Clinchfield #154, a Baldwin-built P-2 Pacific, pulls a short passenger consist. Collection of Tom L. Sink.

A Clinchfield E-2 Mallet rolls by on one of the few relatively straight sections of track on the entire line. Courtesy of the North Carolina State Archives.

Clinchfield #731, a 2-8-8-2, was built by Baldwin in 1919. Courtesy of the Pennsylvania Railroad Museum.

title East Tennessee Railway.

In North Carolina the Clinchfield Railroad interchanged with the Black Mountain Railroad at Kona. This short line railroad was, for many years, a subsidiary of the Clinchfield. The railroad's only connection to the outside world was the interchange at Kona. It is currently independent, but has suspended its operations. It is the hope of the current owner to restore service and operate the railroad as a combination freight line and excursion railroad.

At Huntdale, the Caney River Railway interchanged with the Clinchfield Railroad. The railway was owned by the J. M. Buck Lumber Company of Johnson City, Tennessee. The line ran eight miles, from Huntdale to Lewisburg, on a 3' gauge track. The company owned three Climax locomotives and 35 log cars. The railroad lasted until 1908 or 1909.

CANEY RIVER RAILWAY.
J. M. BUCK, President and General Passenger Agt., Johnson City, Tenn.
Extends from Huntdale to **Bald Mountain**,[1] N.C., a distance of 20 miles. Operated on irregular schedule for freight and passenger traffic.
Connection.—[1] With South & Western Ry.   *March*, 1905.

The Caney River Railway was for all intents and purposes a logging railroad with three Climax locomotives. Courtesy of *The Official Railway Guide*.

The Dibell Mineral Company ordered a new Shay, c/n 3175 in 1922. The railroad ran from the Dibell Mines to the CC&O at Penland, a distance of approximately eight miles on a 3' gauge track. Carolina Mineral bought the line in 1930, and mining continued until the mid-1930s. The principal mineral mined was feldspar, which, after being cleaned and crushed, had detergent added to become Bon Ami cleanser.

Tennessee Eastman operated a 3' gauge railroad line out of Altapass, North Carolina. The purpose of the line was to collect acid wood along the route. The sole motive power was a Class "A" Shay, c/n 2814. The rail was removed in 1933.

The T. T. Adams Company operated a 3' gauge line in McDowell County. The connection with the CC&O was at Sevier, North Carolina. The line was laid in 40-pound rail and extended 12 miles. The motive power was a single Climax locomotive.

At Marion, North Carolina, a connection was made with the Southern Railway at "Clinchcross."

The Clinchfield Railroad interchanged with the Seaboard Air Line Railroad at Bostic, North Carolina. It appeared for a while that the Clinchfield would terminate at Bostic, but it later pushed on to Spartanburg, South Carolina. Spartanburg became the southern terminus for the Clinchfield, and there it interchanged with the Southern Railway, the Piedmont & Northern Railroad, and the Seaboard Air Line Railroad.

The major mergers of the late 1970s and early 1980s swept the Clinchfield Railroad up into the corporate consolidations which characterized the period. Today, the railroad plays a major role in the operations of the CSX Transportation Corporation. The Chesapeake & Ohio, Piedmont & Northern, and

An E-2 class, 4-6-6-4 simple articulated #660 sits on a pass track for a meet with engine #805. The location is Marion, North Carolina, on June 26, 1946. Collection of Tom Wicker.

On June 26, 1949, an F3A, #805 passes #660, a 4-6-6-4 Challenger, near Marion, North Carolina. Photograph by David Driscoll.

Caney River Railway #377, a Class "A" Climax with its distinctive T-shaped boiler, is photographed near Lewisburg, North Carolina. Collection of Jody Higgins.

Lima Locomotive Company #3175 was a two-truck Shay built for the Dibell Mineral Company of Penland, North Carolina. The locomotive was constructed on February 9, 1922. Courtesy of the Allen County Historical Society, Lima, Ohio.

The Dibell Mineral Co. #1 interchanges with the CC&O Railway at Penland, North Carolina. The #1, c/n 3175, was a 3' gauge Shay built in February 1922 for the Dibell Mineral Company. Collection of Frank Moore.

The Tennessee Eastman #56 is photographed in approximately 1932 at Altapass, North Carolina. The railroad was used to bring acid wood from Honeycutt Ridge to a connection with the Clinchfield at Altapass. The two-truck, two-cylinder Shay, c/n 2814, was constructed in July 1915 by the Lima Locomotive Works. The large rocks in the tender were coal, which had to be broken up by the crew with a sledgehammer in order to fire the locomotive. Collection of Lee Medford.

T.T. Adams Company #1 is shown in Sevier, North Carolina, in 1914. The locomotive was used to haul acid wood to a connection on the CC&O at Sevier. Collection of C.K. Marsh, Jr.

F-7 #809 is on the pass track below the Blue Ridge Tunnel. The date is September 1970. Photograph by Tom L. Sink.

Clinchfield Locomotive Classification	
Wheel Configuration	Class
2-6-0	F
2-8-0	H
2-8-2	K
4-4-0	D
4-6-0	G
4-6-2	P
2-6-6-2	M
2-8-8-2	L
4-6-6-4	E

The Clinchfield A-A-B-B-A set led by #805 rumbles through Western North Carolina. Photograph by J.H. Wade. Collection of Frank Ardrey.

Clinchfield #3600 at the old engine facility in Erwin, Tennessee. The Clinchfield bought only eight U36-Cs and quickly traded the units to the Seaboard Coast Line Railroad for SD-45s. This was the Clinchfield's only excursion into GE-produced locomotives. Photograph by Tom L. Sink.

Seaboard Air Line railroads have become part of the CSX Railroad System. The Norfolk & Western and the Southern (which absorbed the Interstate) have merged into the Norfolk Southern Corporation. This leaves only two large megarailroads in the southeastern United States.

Despite the many failed and aborted attempts to establish the Clinchfield Railroad, it should be noted the 277-mile section of tracks which eventually became that railroad has been absorbed into the CSX Railroad System in its entirety.

After the Clinchfield dieselized, helpers were still needed to help move the tonnage up the Loops. In the photograph above, the pushers, including two B-units, are shown in Spruce Pine, North Carolina. Collection of Tom L. Sink.

GP-9 #901 emerges from the Blue Ridge Tunnel on Labor Day Weekend, 1970. Photograph by Tom L. Sink.

THE BLACK MOUNTAIN RAILROAD & THE YANCEY RAILROAD

For many years, the Black Mountain Railroad enjoyed a close relationship with the Clinchfield Railroad. In the early 1900s, when the Clinchfield was constructed along the banks of the Toe River, a decision was made to push south on a branchline to Micaville and then on to Bowditch. The line was privately funded for only the first couple of years. After that point, it became one of the few subsidiaries of the Clinchfield Railroad.

In approximately 1907, construction began from Kona, North Carolina, to Micaville and Bowditch. In 1912 the tracks had reached Burnsville, and in 1913 they had reached Eskota, North Carolina, near the base of Mount Mitchell. Mount Mitchell, the highest point east of the Rockies, has an elevation of 6,638 feet. Mount Mitchell and Mount Celo, both in the general vicinity of the railroad, are part of the Black Mountain Range, hence the origin of the railroad's name.

At its height of operations, which spanned the years between 1913 and 1928, the line stretched over 23 miles, from Eskota to Kona. The line from Eskota to Burnsville, utilized primarily for the removal of timber, marked the zenith of prosperity for the line. After 1928, when the timber was depleted, the line between Eskota and Burnsville was removed. County Road 197 is now paved on top of the original railroad bed.

While the railroad was completing the construction of the rails from Kona to Eskota, two lumber companies proceeded with the acquisition of timber rights in the area. The first was the Carolina Spruce Company, which held timber rights to 5,200 acres and established a single-band sawmill at Pensacola. Nearby, a tract of 13,000 acres was controlled by Brown Brothers and Associates, who had built a double-band sawmill a mile farther south, at Murchison. Using switchbacks, the Brown interests built a standard gauge line which ran halfway up the northern slope of Mount Mitchell. Other portions of Mount Mitchell were being timbered by the Perley & Crockett operation, which shipped its timber south with a connection with the Southern Railway near Ridgecrest, North Carolina.

Before World War I, a labor shortage developed. To continue the increased spruce production, the mills were forced to hire immigrant labor. At one time, the immigrant labor force numbered close to 400 Austrian and Italian workers. The workers were recalled shortly after the outbreak of the war; however, the need for spruce only accelerated. The light, yet resilient spruce was necessary for the construction of aircraft wings and fuselages. The federal government was so concerned about the production of spruce that it implemented extreme measures to insure its availability. One such measure was to order the Mount Mitchell Railroad, the Perley & Crockett operation, to cease its excursion business and concentrate solely on spruce timbering.

Daily passenger service on the Black Mountain Railroad included a mixed train which left Murchison at 9:30 a.m. and picked up passengers along the route to Kona. Reversing its route, the train arrived back at Murchison around 5:20 p.m. The round-trip was approximately 46 miles in length.

The Black Mountain Railroad had two notable wrecks which are part of the local folklore. Both wrecks involved the three-truck Shay, the #2, which had arrived on the railroad in 1914.

The first wreck occurred outside of Burnsville, where the line swings south toward Pensacola. The wreck occurred when a string of loaded log cars broke loose and began rolling down the grade toward Burnsville. Simultaniously, the crew of engine #2 pulled out of Burnsville on their trip to Pensacola. As the engine rolled out of Burnsville, it was met by the runaway log cars. In the ensuing crash, Engineer Otis Mumpower was scalded to death, and his father, Bill Mumpower, was severely injured.

The story of the second wreck, as it has been retold by the local residents, is the substance of pure folklore. It was standard practice for the train crew to make two round-trips per day from Pensacola to Burnsville. The crews hauled cut lumber north to Burnsville, and hauled logging camp supplies and general merchandise south to Pensacola.

On one particular day, Engineer Paul Darty had his heart set on courting later in the evening. In order to keep his appointment for later in the day, he made

The first passenger train into Pensacola, North Carolina, arrived in 1915. The wooden Black Mountain Railroad combine was pushed by the Clinchfield #6. The #6 was a Baldwin-built 4-6-0 which was constructed in June 1882 for the Shenandoah Valley Railroad as its #40. The locomotive then went to the Norfolk & Western as its #547, to the Lick Creek & Lake Erie as its #6, to the South & Western Railway as its #6, and finally to the CC&O as its #6. Collection of Jody Higgins.

The Carolina Spruce Company was a standard gauge operation which ran from Pensacola, North Carolina, to the foot of Mount Mitchell. The Carolina Spruce Company #1 was a Shay, built in April 1913, c/n 2670, and was photographed with an American log loader near Pensacola, North Carolina. Collection of Jody Higgins.

The Brown Brothers Lumber Company operated a narrow gauge logging operation which timbered the lower slopes of Mount Mitchell. The Eskota, North Carolina, mill marked the southernmost community served by the Black Mountain Railroad. Collection of Jody Higgins.

A Perley & Crockett Lumber Company Climax is photographed on the north slope of Mount Mitchell, part of the Black Mountain Range. Collection of Jody Higgins.

Former CC&O #99, now the Black Mountain Railroad #3, sits outside the Burnsville station. As of 1993, the station still stands but sits abandoned behind a local building supply company. Collection of Jody Hig-

The Black Mountain #2 was a 36-ton Lima-built three-truck Shay, c/n 2798. Originally constructed in 1914, the #2 served on the Black Mountain Railroad until 1928, when it was leased to the Vrendenburgh Sawmill in Corduroy, Alabama. Collection of Jody Higgins.

the customary two trips in record time. The mill supervisor at Pensacola insisted on a third round-trip, since plenty of daylight existed. After a heated exchange, Engineer Darty made a vow that he would "return by four p.m. or run this train to hell!" Witnesses remembered the Shay ran at an extremely high rate of speed on the down grade from Pensacola to Burnsville. The witnesses also stated the screeching of the flanges was constant and sounded in some ways like music. As the train rounded a sharp curve, the engine left the tracks and pitched into the hollow below. The escaping steam shot hundreds of feet into the sky after the locomotive finally came to rest. The engineer was killed instantly, but the camp physician, Dr. Smith, and another railroad engineer, Mr. Corbin, while severely injured, survived the wreck.

The engineer's body was recovered but remained unburied at the local barber shop so that family members could make arrangements for the funeral. After a telegram went unanswered for seven days,

the body was finally put to rest. A day after the burial, Darty's brother arrived from Pennsylvania with a steel-lined casket. The body was exhumed and placed in the casket, and thus began a slow journey back to Pennsylvania for burial in his home state. An immigrant worker who died shortly afterward in an unrelated accident soon occupied the empty grave.

By the early 1920s, the mills at Pensacola and Murchison depleted the timber reserves and the railroad began to curtail services. In 1926 both passenger and mail service were suspended, and in 1928 the line was abandoned altogether. The rails were removed later that same year between Eskota and Burnsville.

On the remainder of the line, traffic was reduced so steadily over the next two decades that in 1951 the Clinchfield Railroad applied for abandonment with the ICC. Permission was granted with one clause: If local interests wished to purchase and operate the line, the Clinchfield Railroad was obligated to sell the

The Black Mountain Railroad Shay #2 is overturned in Yancey County, North Carolina. This wreck resulted in the death of Engineer Paul Darty and the severe injury of the camp doctor and a second locomotive engineer. Collection of Jody Higgins.

This wreck on the Black Mountain Railroad resulted in a fatality, Mr. William (Bill) Dodson. The wreck occurred just outside Micaville, North Carolina. Collection of Jody Higgins.

CC&O #99 became the Black Mountain Railroad #3 and is photographed in Burnsville, North Carolina, in September 1951. Collection of Harold K. Vollrath.

The Black Mountain Railroad water tower in Burnsville, North Carolina, during a severe cold spell in January 1953. The #99, later the #3, is in the background. Photograph by Doug Walker.

With a brakeman keeping an eye open at road crossings, the #3 pushes two boxcars down the line. Collection of Tom L. Sink.

line to the local interests at a fair market value.

Local interests stepped forward and raised $70,000 to obtain the line from the Clinchfield Railroad. The selling price was negotiated to $22,000, which allowed the local interests to have money left over for the purchase of a new GE-built 44-ton switch engine. A small engine shed was erected in

Without benefit of a wye, Black Mountain #3 pushes a cut of cars towards Micaville. Collection of Tom L. Sink.

The Yancey Railroad #1 is a GE 44-tonner and was photographed in Burnsville, North Carolina, on September 8, 1970. Photograph by J.H. Wade. Collection of Frank Ardrey.

Burnsville, and the railroad was christened the Yancey Railroad in 1955.

The line showed a profit until 1971, when the Feldspar Corporation closed its Bowditch plant. This closing cost the railroad 3,000 tons of freight annually. Another calamity hit in 1972, when Hurricane Agnes moved inland and dumped inches of rain on the local area. The railroad had several bridges washed out, and in some areas the overall track was left in poor shape. Additional flooding in 1977 washed out the entire line between Burnsville and Micaville.

The line held on until the early 1980s, when operations slowly ceased. At this time, a large portion of the tracks was used to store unwanted boxcars from other railroads. As of 1994, the current owners are attempting to reestablish the road crossing at Mica-

Black Mountain #1 was a 4-6-0 built at the Logansport, Indiana, shops in 1882. The locomotive originally went to the Columbus, Chicago & Indiana Central Railroad as the #423, then to the Pittsburgh, Cincinnati & St. Louis Railroad, then to the Ohio River & Charleston Railroad, then to the South & Western, to the Clinchfield, and finally to the Black Mountain Railroad. Photograph by John B. Allen. Collection of Cary F. Poole.

The #2, a GE 45-ton center-cab, was referred to as Puddles. It often was used on the Bowditch section of the line at the feldspar plant. Photograph by Tom L. Sink.

ville. Current motive power is a Vulcan center-cab locomotive. The locomotive, purchased from the Narragansett & Pier Railroad, is stranded on the south side of Highway 19E with only a few hundred feet of track in which to operate.

The remainder of the existing eight miles of track, which stretches north from Micaville to Kona, lies on the north side of Highway 19E. The paving over of the highway in recent years prevents the locomotive from getting to the north side of its tracks.

Although the motive power on the Black Mountain/Yancey Railroad was never extensive, it did have an illustrious history in most cases. In addition to the Shay, the Black Mountain Railroad had two 4-6-0 locomotives, which came from the Clinchfield Railroad.

The main motive power lay with a diminutive 45-ton 4-6-0, which the Black Mountain Railroad labeled as its #1. This particular locomotive had served at least six owners before arriving on the Black Mountain Railroad. The locomotive served until 1953, when it was shipped to Erwin, Tennessee, home shops for the Clinchfield Railroad. After sitting for several years, the #1 was restored by the Clinchfield Railroad for use in the excursion business. The engine served in that capacity until the early 1980s, when a broken main frame forced it into the B&O Museum in Baltimore, Maryland. Here it sits in a place of honor in the rotunda of the roundhouse.

Another engine owned by the Black Mountain Railroad was a much larger 4-6-0 weighing 68 tons. This engine had previously served as the Clinchfield #99. The locomotive served on the newly formed Yancey Railroad as a backup engine to the diesels. After being sent to Erwin for repairs, the locomotive remained there for several years. The locomotive has been preserved at the Casey Jones' Museum in Jackson, Tennessee. The engine has had its builder's plates altered to match the builder's date of Casey Jones' own engine, number 382.

The Black Mountain/Yancey Railroad's modern diesel power consisted initially of three General Electric-built center-cab switchers: a 44-ton, a 45-ton, and a 65 ton. Today, the sole remaining motive power on the line is a rare Vulcan-built center-cab locomotive which is in the 65-ton range.

The #3 was a GE-built 65-ton center-cab locomotive. It was the heaviest motive power used in modern operations on the Yancey Railroad. Photograph by Tom L. Sink.

The sole remaining motive power is a 65-ton Vulcan locomotive. The locomotive has been embargoed from the main part of its line ever since Highway 19E was paved over the tracks. Photograph by Cary F. Poole.

EAST TENNESSEE & WESTERN NORTH CAROLINA RAILROAD
LINVILLE RIVER RAILROAD

The ET&WNC Railroad was a narrow gauge line which developed a loyal following, not only among the local mountain folk who depended upon the line every day, but also among the visitors to the valleys traveled by the line. But while the railroad enjoyed a large degree of popularity due to its passenger and excursion business, the line was initially formed to haul iron ore.

The ET&WNC was chartered on May 24, 1866, and construction began shortly thereafter on a 5' broad gauge line. The original plan was to build a line from Johnson's Depot, now Johnson City, Tennessee, to Cranberry, North Carolina. Only a short section of grading was completed before the original company was found to be delinquent in its debts and was publicly auctioned for $20,000. John Hughes first purchased the line, and Ario Pardee, a Pennsylvania coal magnate, later obtained controlling interest.

Prior to the purchase of the ET&WNC, Pardee had acquired the Cranberry Iron Works. His intent was to conclude the grading and laying of rails to help facilitate the removal of the iron ore around Cranberry. The ore deposits in that area were some of the purest yet discovered in the eastern United States. By 1879 construction began in earnest, but Pardee was an avid narrow gauge proponent, and the line was re-configured to be a 3' gauge. Pardee felt the benefits of the narrow gauge—lighter rail and smaller equipment—were ideal for the mountainous terrain to be served by the railroad.

One formidable obstacle the ET&WNC had to overcome was the Blue Ridge Mountains, in which no railroad had yet been successful. From Hampton, Tennessee, at the mouth of the Doe River Gorge, to Cranberry, North Carolina, the line climbed over 1,500 feet in elevation. Many of the cuts had to be hand chiseled and blown out by dynamite in order to construct the roadbed. In the Doe River Gorge, construction was hampered by the sheer steepness of the gorge walls and the general inaccessibility of the area. To help facilitate the construction of the line in the gorge, mules, men, and supplies were lowered by slings to the construction sites. By 1881, 15 years after the charter was issued, the line stretched 34 miles, from Johnson City to Cranberry. It was estimated the construction costs had exceeded $1 million.

Ario Pardee was also a member of the controlling

Engineer Sherman Pippen has his picture taken in a classical pose as he "oils around" engine #12. Photograph by R.F. Harding. Collection of C.K. Marsh, Jr.

An excursion train poses in the Doe River Gorge during an outing. Photograph by R.F. Harding. Collection of C.K. Marsh, Jr.

interests of the East Broad Top Railway of Orbisonia, Pennsylvania. This railroad, also a 3' narrow gauge, operated in south-central Pennsylvania. Until the demise of the ET&WNC and the East Broad Top, both lines retained a common board member.

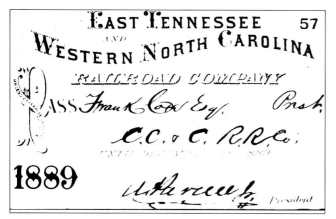

In 1889, the ET&WNC Railroad issued a pass to Frank Coxe, president of the Charleston, Cincinnati & Chicago Railroad (later the Clinchfield Railroad). Courtesy of UNC-Asheville.

From the late 1860s to the mid-1890s, a wave of narrow gauge fever swept the United States. Three men were largely responsible for the explosion of narrow gauge projects in the latter part of the nineteenth century. The first was General William Jackson Palmer, who created the Denver & Rio Grande Railway in Colorado. The Denver & Rio Grande was a fairly large system, which promoted the idea that narrow gauge railroads did not necessarily have to be relegated to short line status.

The second gentleman, Colonel Edward Hulbert, was the primary proponent of narrow gauge lines in the South. Hulbert promoted his belief in the narrow gauge system through a pamphlet, "The Narrow Gauge Railway," and by hosting the 1872 and 1878 narrow gauge conventions. Through the pamphlet and by hosting the conventions, his fame throughout the South soon convinced other railroad officials to consider narrow gauge construction. One of the major arguments for narrow gauge construction was in the economics and capital savings due to lower costs involved in the purchasing of equipment and construction of the roadbed. Due to the lack of expendable capital in the South after the Civil War, the narrow gauge principle seemed logical. Hulbert used the savings in costs in his arguments, and his comments were warmly received.

The third gentleman who helped spread the narrow gauge movement was a Scotsman named Robert F. Fairlie. His ideas centered on the fact that he felt weight on most locomotives was poorly distributed on the lead and trailing trucks, and he felt constructing equipment with driving wheels only was the most efficient use of the narrow gauge principles. His beliefs ran as far as redesigning turntables and bridges and adjusting rail weight to economize on the savings of weight. Weight, he rationalized, could only promote the narrow gauge cause in a positive fashion. Eventually, most of his theories proved to be unfounded, although some of his locomotive designs became popular in Europe.

The movement escalated when a convention was organized in St. Louis, Missouri, in 1872. Colonel Hulbert was instrumental in inviting represenatives of most of the current narrow gauge lines to the convention. For two days those in attendance were regaled with stories of success from various narrow gauge projects. Another convention was planned for 1878.

The movement peaked in the late 1870s when the depression of that period forced most railroad construction to be affected by the declining economy. This depression lasted for a period of five years. In 1876 narrow gauge construction reached its highest pinnacle when it accounted for 35% of all railroad construction. The percentage then tapered off dramatically, and between 1885 and 1886 dropped from 17% to 6.8%. The fever was truly over, but pro-

jects currently under construction continued, as did the ET&WNC. Ario Pardee was a loyal convert who could not be swayed otherwise and remained committed to narrow gauge construction.

With the line completed from Johnson City, Tennessee, to Cranberry, North Carolina, by the Cranberry Iron & Coal Company, the day-to-day operations of the line were turned over to Ario Pardee, Jr. The line was officially opened on July 3, 1882, with mixed passenger and freight traffic between the two terminal points. The small blast furnace at Cranberry was capable initially of processing 14 to 15 tons of ore per day. The finished iron was sent to Ohio and Pennsylvania, where it was used in the manufacturing of tool-grade steel.

On July 13, 1896, the three Camp brothers, early loggers who first worked the area, incorporated a railroad which would connect with the ET&WNC at Cranberry and extend 12 miles to Saginaw, North Carolina, now referred to as Pineola. After the construction of a hotel and some minor grading, the railroad project fell into debt. With the Camp brothers' interests up for public auction, W. M. Ritter and his associates purchased the assets for $12,000.

A Class "A" Climax locomotive belonging to Hutton, Bourbonnais & Company crosses Wilson Creek at Hutbow, North Carolina. Collection of Doug Walker.

A W.M. Ritter Company Class "A" Climax locomotive is photographed at the Saginaw (Pineola) mill in 1904. Collection of Doug Walker.

In 1899 Ritter and an associate, Isaac T. Mann, incorporated the Linville River Railroad. Track laying resumed and completion was expected by May of that year. The Ritter operations were based in Pineola, with the old Brown Brothers mill being used to cut ties and bridge timbers for the new railroad. Track was laid in 33-pound rail, and soon tracks radiated from Pineola in several directions.

The ET&WNC and the Linville River railroads were often referred to solely as narrow gauge lines. In truth, the ET&WNC Railroad had the section of track from Johnson City to Elizabethton converted to dual gauge in 1904. The job of adding the third rail was later extended to a new Ritter operation which had started at Hampton. This extension was completed by 1910. The narrow gauge locomotives provided the motive power, but they were often seen shifting and sorting standard gauge cars. In 1903 the ET&WNC converted to knuckle couplers, away from the old and dangerous link-and-pin couplers. A new swinging coupler device was designed to allow the coupler to align on the center line of the standard gauge cars or to swing back to its original position for narrow gauge cars. The railroad applied for and received a U.S. Patent Office license for the device. The railroad's willingness to dual gauge the track between Johnson City and Hampton helps to illustrate the long association between the ET&WNC and the W. M. Ritter Company.

Limited passenger service was offered on the Linville River Railroad with the addition of a coach lettered #1. The W. M. Ritter Company held company picnics, and one of its Climax locomotives often pulled the coach for the excursions.

By 1912 the timber reserves were beginning to diminish. At that time, the W. M. Ritter Company began transferring equipment from the Pineola operation to a new operation which had been estab-

The crew on the #3 poses with their locomotive in Johnson City, Tennessee. The #3 was a 2-8-0 constructed by the Baldwin Locomotive Works in 1882. Collection of C.K. Marsh, Jr.

The crew of ET&WNC #6 poses in the snow in Newland, North Carolina, in 1914. Collection of Harold K. Vollrath.

The W.M. Ritter Company held an outing in 1902 using their own narrow gauge Climax locomotive, #2, and a Linville River Railroad coach. Collection of Lee Medford.

lished at Mortimer on the Carolina & North-Western Railway. This transfer of equipment was accomplished by a set of temporary rails which ran up Lost Cove Creek. After completion of the transfer of equipment, the line was removed.

With Ritter now out of operations as far as its Pineola office was concerned, the company had little need for the Linville Railroad. On August 1, 1913, the sale of the railroad was concluded and the ET&WNC took possession of the 12 miles of track. With the bill of sale also came various pieces of rolling stock and locomotives, some of which were in various stages of disrepair.

In 1915 a mill was established at Shulls Mills by William S. Whiting. In negotiations with the management of the ET&WNC, Whiting asked for an extension from Pineola to Shulls Mills.

It took a vote of stockholders, but on July 14, 1915, the required vote was obtained, and construction soon started on an additional 14 miles of track. A decision was made to start the construction at Montezuma, which left Pineola on a spur rather than the main line.

In the meantime, William Whiting had incorporated his timber holdings and had formed the Boone Fork Lumber Company at Shulls Mills. As the line was being completed to Shulls Mills, a new mill was also under construction. In September of 1916, the extension was completed.

With the end-of-track only eight miles from Boone, North Carolina, site of Appalachian State Normal College, the ET&WNC was soon approached for another extension. In order to entice the railroad to construct the line into Boone, a bond referendum resulted in the raising of $27,000 to be used in the construction.

The ET&WNC, through its subsidiary, the Linville River Railroad, now had a decision on its hands. The citizens of Banner Elk had also requested an extension to their community. With the passage of the bond issue by the people of Boone, the railroad knew its decision was to press on to that city. The extension into Boone would give the railroad a total of 66 miles of track. Work commenced on March 21, 1918, and crews of over 200 men spent the next seven months constructing the eight miles to join Boone with Shulls Mills. The work concluded when locomotive #4 arrived in Boone on October 24, 1918.

The Boone Fork Lumber Company is photographed circa 1914 at Shulls Mills, North Carolina. The photograph shows a Class "A" Climax parked and another similar locomotive pulling a string of log cars. Collection of Doug Walker.

A celebration occurred in Boone, North Carolina, during the autumn of 1918. The first train of the Linville River Railroad had finally reached Boone. Collection of Doug Walker.

To celebrate the arrival of the line, the city of Boone held a tremendous celebration. The community was now connected to the outside world. The mayor of Banner Elk, the community which lost out to Boone, was also present at the celebration. When asked to give a speech and add to the festivities, Mayor Shull stood, approached the podium, and delivered a memorable one-line speech. He said, "I remember when the only way a person could get to Boone was to be born in Boone," and promptly sat down.

The ET&WNC was well-known for its passenger service, and equipped its line with vestibule coaches and parlor cars. These coaches were known as some of the finest to grace any railroad, standard or narrow gauge. The railroad even boasted through some of its brochures to have THE finest passenger service. The railroad owned a parlor car named the *Azalea*, which was truly an ornate coach. This particular coach was constructed by the Jackson & Sharp Company. The *Azalea* served the line for many years but was finally retired in 1935. It later served the United Fruit Company in Central America. Passenger service consisted of round-trips between Johnson City, Tennessee, and Boone, North Carolina, over the line's 66 miles of track.

The ET&WNC also constructed four excursion cars in its home shops to meet the demands of an ever burgeoning sight-seeing business. These cars were largely retired in the late 1930s.

Despite its passenger service, the ET&WNC had been founded under the guise of an ore carrier. Initially, the iron ore was processed at Cranberry; but later, part of the ore was processed at the Virginia

An early photograph shows an ET&WNC train passing through the Doe River Gorge near Hampton, Tennessee. Collection of Hugh Morton.

The #14 is photographed in Johnson City, Tennessee, in the late 1930s. Included in the mixed freight is one of the piggyback cars of the ET&WNC. The #14 was built new for the ET&WNC by Baldwin in 1919. Collection of Doug Walker.

Iron, Coal & Coke Company of Johnson City, Tennessee. The railroad had a unique dual gauge transfer system at Johnson City. Both coal, which was headed toward Cranberry, and iron ore, arriving from Cranberry, were handled by this transfer facility. If coal was needed in Cranberry, the standard gauge cars unloaded into the narrow gauge cars, which were positioned below. If ore needed to be delivered to the standard gauge cars, the narrow gauge cars were on the top of the transfer. In 1906 the Cranberry furnace was closed, and operations were shifted totally to the Virginia Iron Company after the acquisition of that firm by the Cranberry Iron & Coal Company. This forced the movement of the ore along the entire length of the line.

The coming of World War I helped to stimulate the ore hauling business, which had begun to fade just

The #12 takes on water while flying "extra" flags. Photograph by R.F. Harding. Collection of C.K. Marsh, Jr.

The #9 posed for its builder's photograph in April 1911. The locomotive had 45" drivers and 15"3 22" cylinders. Courtesy of the Railroad Museum of Pennsylvania.

prior to the war. After the armistice was signed, the ore business was down again, and the mine closed temporarily in 1921. It reopened two years later but held on only until 1929, at which time it was permanently closed.

After the ore business and most of the timbering reserves were exhausted, the ET&WNC was helped to stay solvent by the hauling of a new commodity—acid wood. Acid wood is chestnut, which contains a high degree of tannic acid. This acid is used in the tanning of leather products. By developing the acid wood business along its route, the railroad tapped a new source of revenue, which, especially during the Depression of the 1930s, was desperately needed.

The ET&WNC, like many short lines, had many monikers placed on it. Some were flattering, some not so complimentary. One of the earliest nicknames was the "Stemwinder," a name which Shepherd M. Dugger placed on the railroad in 1890. He compared the punctuality and fine-tuned operation of the line to the "best jewelled stemwinder in the pocket of the millionaire."

The #12 pulls a load of acid wood near Cranberry in 1942. Collection of Doug Walker.

ET&WNC #7 was the only narrow gauge 0-8-0 built. It was constructed by the Brooks Locomotive Company. The #7 was photographed in Johnson City, Tennessee, on February 14, 1935. Photograph by John B. Allen. Collection of Cary F. Poole.

A second nickname brought some humor to the railroad during a period when some humor was sorely needed—the Great Depression. With the abject poverty of Appalachia, particularly during the 1930s, the letters ET&WNC were comically referred to as "Eat Taters and Wear No Clothes." It was often joked that Cy Crumley, a long-time railroad employee, had a quick comeback to the above nickname by referring to the same letters as standing for "Every Trip With No Complaints" or "Exquisite Trains and What Nice Conductors."

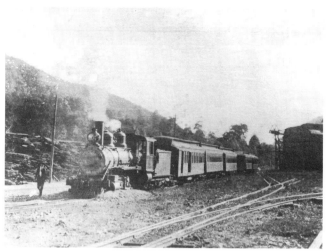

An early photograph shows engine #8 at Cranberry, North Carolina. The #8 was a Baldwin-built 4-6-0 which was constructed in 1907 and later was sold to the Gray Lumber Company of Waverly, Virginia. Collection of C.K. Marsh, Jr.

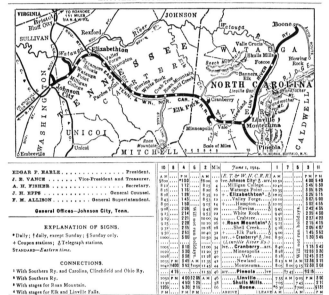

The 1924 *Official Railway Guide* lists the stations along the route of the ET&WNC, which stretched to its fullest length of 66 miles.

The most common nickname was simple: "Tweetsie." It is a frequent misconception that the local population originated the nickname Tweetsie. The fact is that visitors, or flatlanders, originated the name because of the shrill sound of the whistle in the mountain valleys. It is ironic that a name originated by outsiders is the most common of the nicknames to survive.

In order to originate other revenue sources, the ET&WNC was involved in both the bus and the trucking industries. In December 1926 the ET&WNC Transportation Company was formed to launch a bus company. With the new roads being constructed during the boom of the automobile era, the company rationalized it could establish a new market. This decision only further weakened the overall passenger business for the railroad, and the problem increased

An excursion train at Cranberry, North Carolina, is headed by #9. The #9 was constructed by Baldwin in 1911 and served both the Linville River Railroad and the ET&WNC Railroad. Collection of Doug Walker.

when the railroad section of the company raised passenger rates with the hope of encouraging customers to try the bus. After a few years, the bus portion of the company was sold, but the damage was already complete: vital customers had been run off.

The railroad also launched a truck-hauling business, which fared a little better. This line survived until recent times and was merged into the Red Ball Express company. The ET&WNC was one of the few narrow gauge short lines to enter the piggyback trailer business. The railroad had four specially designed flatcars which had depressed sides. This depression was where the rear wheels of the trailer rested, and the result was a lowered overall height of the flatcar and the semitrailer body. The lowered height helped the load pass through the tunnels along the route.

Flatcar #300 was one of the cars specially designed to carry truck trailers. The design allowed the overall height to be lowered, thus allowing the trailer roofs to clear the tunnels on the railroad. Photograph by People's Studios. Collection of Frank

The line was often referred to as one of the most spectacular narrow gauge rides in the entire country. One of the highlights of the trip was the Doe River Gorge. The gorge that had required mules used in construction to be lowered by slings was a spectacle for every rider who was given the privilege to travel its length. At Pardee Point in the gorge, passengers could look straight down a vertical rock wall to the river raging below.

One of the quaint communities served by the ET&WNC was the summer resort village of Linville, North Carolina. The community was known for its distinctive architectural style, which utilized the bark of the chestnut tree for exterior siding. Before the devastating chestnut blight, the tree was extremely plentiful and furnished an inexpensive source for the siding. One of the proponents of the bark siding was Henry Bacon, designer of the Lincoln Memorial in Washington, DC. The Linville depot, which employed the chestnut bark for its exterior siding, greeted many of the thousands of passengers who passed through the area.

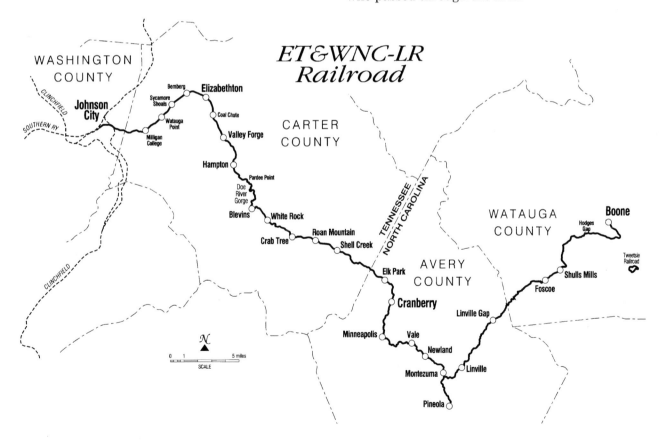

The full extent of the line from Johnson City, Tennessee, to Boone, North Carolina, is illustrated in the map above. The map also includes the approximate location of the modern-day Tweetsie amusement park, operator of the #12, the last of the ET&WNC locomotives. Courtesy of Chris Ford.

Many short lines had employees who remained loyal to their railroads for the entire duration of their working careers, and the ET&WNC was no exception. One employee who appeared bigger than life was Charles Glover "Cy" Crumley. He joined the railroad on August 15, 1906, and continued with the same employer for the next 54 years. In this tolerant, considerate man, the ET&WNC found a ready source to market its cause, whether as a salesman or kindly conductor. Crumley was the spokesman for the railroad when he appeared on a national talk show based out of New York City called *We the People*. By this time, narrow gauge railroads were somewhat of a rarity, and his appearance centered on the mountain culture and how the railroad provided a means of communication and transportation for the mountain communities. He also figured prominently in a silent newsreel of the late 1930s titled *Tennessee Tweetsie*.

Even on a day-to-day basis, Crumley plugged the short line in his duties. When passengers were short on fare, he was often overheard saying, "We're going there anyhow." During the Depression, when the entire country was suffering, the line was referred to as the railroad with a heart. Conductor Crumley had a ticket puncher fashioned in the shape of a heart. Cy Crumley was cross-trained to handle a variety of jobs, from engineer to conductor, but public relations may have been his best trade.

The railroad was often plagued by flooding, and the line between Cranberry and Boone was one of the sections most prone. One of the worst floods occurred

A young lady peeks at #11 from the Cranberry, North Carolina, depot on August 9, 1941. Photograph by G.W. Pettengill. Collection of C.K. Marsh, Jr.

A mixed train headed by #11 travels eastbound from Hampton, Tennessee, to Elk Park, North Carolina. Collection of Harold K. Vollrath.

in 1940 and destroyed much of the track between Cranberry and Boone. Since revenues had been down for some time, the decision was made not to rebuild the line. A howl of opposition was made by the local residents, who would be left without rail service if the plan to close the line went through. However, the decision to abandon was approved on March 22, 1941.

The decision to abandon the Linville section left only the dual gauge section between Johnson City and Elizabethton and the narrow gauge section on to Cranberry. In September 1950 a proposal to abandon the remaining narrow gauge line was approved, and the last run on the line occurred October 16, 1950.

As of 1994, there are two distinct and separate remnants of the ET&WNC. First, the narrow gauge locomotive #12 survives in an amusement park aptly named "Tweetsie," located near Blowing Rock, North

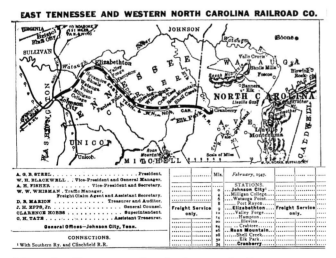

After the disastrous flood of 1940, the line was curtailed to Cranberry, North Carolina. Courtesy of *The Official Railway Guide*.

A mixed freight pulls out ahead of a passenger train in Elk Park, North Carolina, during the early 1940s. Collection of Doug Walker.

The last eastbound train on the East Tennessee & Western North Carolina Railroad. The date is October 16, 1950. The honors were given to #11, a Baldwin locomotive built in 1916 and scrapped in 1952. Collection of Doug Walker.

The #204, c/n 6239, was a standard gauge 2-8-0 Consolidation originally built by Lima in 1922 for the Alabama, Tennessee & Northern Railroad. The locomotive was scrapped in 1955. Photograph by John B. Allen. Collection of Cary F. Poole.

Carolina. The shop crew at Tweetsie expertly cares for the locomotive, and it was placed on the National Registar of Historic Places in the summer of 1992 to celebrate its 75th birthday.

The other remnant is the portion of the line between Johnson City and Elizabethton. Still operated as a standard gauge short line, its current name is the East Tennessee Railway. It provides switching duty for the two terminal points. The railroad operates two ALCO RS-32 diesel locomotives. The old engine shed which once housed the ET&WNC steam locomotives still exists and now houses the ALCO diesels.

ET&WNC #208, ex-Southern Railway engine #630, is in service at the Bemberg Plant near Elizabethton, Tennessee. Photograph by Tom L. Sink.

The youngsters in the photograph are from Camp Yonahnoka, Linville, North Carolina. The camp was created in the 1920s, and from that time on, until the demise of the ET&WNC, the campers went on an overnight hike by riding the train from Linville to Linville Gap. There they would camp for the night, and the next day the youngest campers rode the train back to Linville while the older campers hiked back. The youngsters are posed with the #12 at Tweetsie Railroad. Collection of Hugh Morton.

The ET&WNC engines #207 and 208 are preparing for the 1960 National Historic Railway Society fan trip. Photograph by Tom L. Sink.

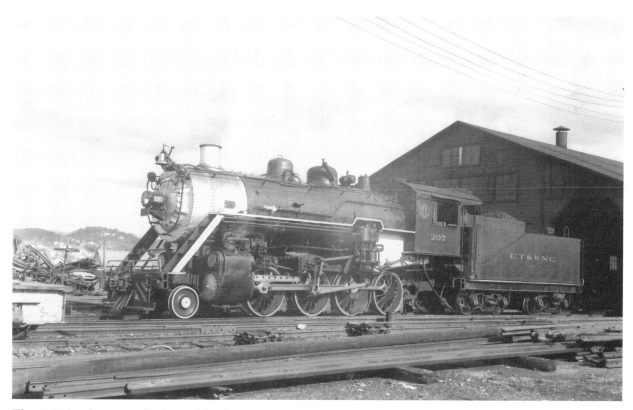

The #207 is photographed outside the engine shed which has served the ET&WNC for many years. The date is March 1961. Photograph by Tom L. Sink.

ET&WNC #209 and #210 were traded to the railroad in exchange for the steam engines #208 and #207. Southern wished to return the steam engines to excursion service. Photographs by Tom L.

MARIETTA AND NORTH GEORGIA RAILROAD

The Marietta and North Georgia Railroad was the Louisville & Nashville predecessor which had an extension from Blue Ridge, Georgia, to Murphy, North Carolina. The M&NG would eventually become part of a 230-mile route from Marietta, Georgia, through Blue Ridge, Georgia, to Knoxville, Tennessee. The name M&NG was used prior to 1896; after that date, the name was changed to the Atlanta, Knoxville & Northern Railroad. In 1902 the line was purchased by the L&N and was referred to by that corporate name.

The original plan for the railroad called for the development of marble quarries in North Georgia and North Carolina and for iron extraction from pits around the Murphy area. In addition to the marble and iron, copper was later extracted from the Ducktown, Tennessee, area.

Originally, the M&NG was constructed as a 3' narrow gauge. The initial plan was to build a line from Marietta to Blue Ridge, on to Murphy, and extend the line through the mountains of Western North Carolina. In some areas, particularly north of Canton, Georgia, the ties were laid in standard gauge fashion. This was done possibly in anticipation of an early conversion from narrow gauge to standard gauge.

The Baldwin-built #4 was a 4-6-0 named the *Frank Siddall*. The locomotive was constructed in 1884 for the 3' narrow gauge railroad. Courtesy of the Pennsylvania Railroad Museum.

The #6 was named the *Evan Howell* and was a narrow gauge 4-6-0 constructed in 1886. Courtesy of the Railroad Museum of Pennsylvania.

An 1889 pass on the Marietta and North Georgia was issued to Frank Coxe, president of the Triple C Railroad. The Triple C was later to become the Clinchfield Railroad. Courtesy of Ramsey Library, UNC-Asheville.

During the 1880s, however, the idea was conceived to construct an alternative route utilizing most of the line from Marietta to Blue Ridge and on to Knoxville. The line was converted to standard gauge, first by utilizing a third rail so both standard and narrow gauge trains could run simultaneously.

The line was completed from Marietta to Knoxville in 1890. Connections on to Atlanta from Marietta were made on the Western and Atlantic Railroad.

The Marietta & North Georgia Railroad entered into immediate receivership, with J. B. Glover appointed as the receiver. Glover was known in the Marietta area as an industrialist who championed the rail service into the local area. Glover's own company later became a manufacturer of industrial locomo-

The Marietta & North Georgia #2, named the *Anelka*, was a 0-4-0 tank engine constructed in 1884 by the Baldwin Locomotive Company. Courtesy of the Railroad Museum of Pennsylvania.

tives and survived as a builder of steam engines well into the 1920s.

The financing for the Marietta & North Georgia often was murky at best. Correspondence from George Eager to J. C. Luterall on November 20, 1894, summed up many of the frustrations. Eager reported that marble production was up and the Ducktown Sulphur & Copper & Iron Company had doubled its production. On the negative side, however, Eager indicated that the trackage was in very poor shape and no investors were interested in the railroad. He further commented that the transfer of the receivership had been bogged down with no resolution in sight.

Additional correspondence from Tully Cormick to J. D. Probst, both attorneys, further attested to the controversy surrounding the receivership. Cormick noted in the correspondence that taxes owed in both Tennessee and Georgia were estimated to be between $45,000 and $47,000. In addition to the back taxes, the Central National Bank had an outstanding note of $52,000. Cormick further commented that J. B. Glover, the current receiver, was a capable administrator who had kept the line operational, but that he seriously doubted Glover had the connections to raise the needed $100,000 to keep the line open.

An affidavit was entered into the Circuit Court of the Northern District of Georgia in which it was motioned for Newsman Ebb to be appointed co-receiver. Ebb was the principal financier for the Kansas City, Wyandott & Northwestern Railroad out of Kansas. In the affidavit, Mr. W. P. Dear swore that Elias Sum-

merfield, an associate of Ebb's, was a known gambler and that the pair would be a poor financial risk.

Charles Kimball of New Jersey bid $950,000 along with his associates in effort to purchase the line. In March 1896 Kimball and his associates were unable to make their second payment, and the line was up for sale once again.

The Marietta & North Georgia #25 was one of the few standard gauge locomotives built new for the railroad. The locomotive was constructed by Baldwin in 1892 as a 2-8-0 Consolidation. Courtesy of the Pennsylvania Railroad Museum.

The Marietta & North Georgia #6 was built by Baldwin. Many narrow gauge locomotives were equipped with the Eames Power Brake, as was the #6. The diaphragm is readily visible under the cab window, and the muffler is located on the cab roof. A major drawback for the Eames braking system was the longer the train, the less effective the braking mechanism, thus the reason many Eames-equipped locomotives were later converted to Westinghouse brakes. Courtesy of the Pennsylvania Railroad Museum.

The question of receivership was finally quelled when the Marietta & North Georgia Railroad was purchased by the Atlanta, Knoxville & Northern Railroad. This railroad had started a parallel route running from Atlanta to Knoxville and was in a much better financial situation. The arrangement proved to be so financially successful that receivers were dismissed in July 1897.

With the completion of the Atlanta, Knoxville & Northern Railroad, the need for a route through the mountains of Western North Carolina was deemed unnecessary. This relegated the former Marietta & North Georgia line—from Blue Ridge, Georgia, to Murphy, North Carolina—to a branchline with only occasional traffic. The Atlanta, Knoxville & Northern soon realized financial solvency was not the only problem associated with the Marietta & North Georgia Railroad. Operational problems and track work lay ahead.

Two major problems were still to be faced. The first, standardizing the track on the newly created Murphy Branch, was accomplished in November 1897. The second was a need to correct a horrible civil engineering problem near the Hiawassee River. It was at this point on the line that a switchback was installed to allow the track to cross over a mountain.

The switchback limited trains to only a few cars, and any train exceeding this meager number had to be broken apart and reassembled on the other side of the mountain. This practice was acceptable when the Marietta & North Georgia was operating the line with only a handful of businesses on the route. When the Atlanta, Knoxville & Northern assumed control, business suddenly boomed and an alternative to the switchback had to be developed.

An L&N engineer, T. A. Aber, resolved the problem by allowing the track to circle Bald Mountain. Beginning at Appalachia, North Carolina, the tracks circled Bald Mountain and began a 426-foot drop to Farner, Tennessee. The descent was accomplished in only six miles of track. This section of track earned itself the nickname of the "Hook and Eye" route because the track completed a loop and crossed under itself via use of a trestle.

In 1902 the L&N purchased the Atlanta, Knoxville & Northern Railroad in order to obtain a route into Atlanta, Georgia.

A trackage agreement was soon negotiated with the Nashville, Chattanooga & St. Louis (NC&StL) Railroad to allow the L&N access to Atlanta through Marietta. The L&N now had a direct route from Atlanta, Georgia, to Knoxville, Tennessee, with a branch to Murphy, North Carolina. The L&N would later absorb the NC&StL, thus negating the need for such an agreement.

During the flood of 1916, three of the four routes into and out of Asheville, North Carolina, were destroyed. The Marietta and North Georgia (L&N at that time) played a significant role in bringing relief

MARIETTA & NORTH GEORGIA RAILWAY.

J. B. GLOVER, Receiver.
W.B. BRADLEY, Gen. Fht.& Pas Agt., Knoxville, Tenn.
J. A. PRIDE, T. F. & P. A., »
W. D. McFARLAND, Auditor.
F. M. BRADLEY, Trav. Auditor & Gen.Agt.

C. B. LACKES, Master Trains and Car Accountant.
J. B. GLOVER, Jr., Supt. Mot. Power.
M. A. CLAYTON, Road Master, Woodstock, Ga.
General Offices—Marietta, Ga.

	4	2	Mls.	January 15, 1893.	Mls.	1	3		
	P. M.	A.M.		LEAVE] [ARRIVE		P. M.	A. M.		
	†3 35	*8 10		..... Atlanta.....		6 25	10 25		
	†4 40	*9 10	0	..... Marietta¹ .. ♂	204.9	5 20	8 50		
	6 03	9 30	6.0	.....Blackwell's.....	198.9	5 03	8 30		
	5 18	9 45	11.8	......Woodstock.... ♂	193.1	4 48	8 15		
	5 28	9 55	15.7	.......Lebanon... ♂	189.2	4 38	8 05		
	5 34	10 02	17.9	...Holly Springs	187.0	4 32	7 59		
	5 51	10 20	24.2	......Canton,.... ♂	180.7	4 16	7 42		
	6 18	10 48	35.5	......Ball Ground... ♂	169.4	3 50	7 17		
			38.8	.......Nelson...... ♂	166.1	3 43	...		
	6 36	11 05	41.4	......Tate...... ♂	163.5	3 33	6 59		
		11 15	47.0	.......Jasper...... ♂	157.9	3 23			
	7 07	11 33	53.0	...Talking Rock.. ♂	151.9	3 05	6 28		
	7 27	11 50	60.0	.......Tolona.... ♂	144.9	2 48	6 08		
	7 45	12 08	67.2	.......Ellijay ... ♂	137.7	2 31	*5 50		
	P. M.	12 25	73.0	.....White Path.. ♂	131.9	12 15	A.M.		
		‖1255	82.6	..... Blue Ridge....	122.3	1 36			
		1 48	96.0	.......Isabella...... ♂	108.9	12 57			
		1 51	97.9	.....Ocoee...... ♂	107.0	12 54			
		2 00	101.6	.....Ducktown.... ♂	103.3	12 45			
		2 18	109.2	.....Pierce... .	95.7	12 27			
		2 28	112.6	....Thompson.. ♂	92.3	12 17			
		2 47	116.8	......Hiawassee.....	88.1	11 52			
		3 02	121.3	....McFarlands... ♂	83.6	11 38			
		3 26	128.9	......Livingston.....	76.0	11 13			
		3 33	131.1	......Higcon.......	73.8	11 07			
		3 45	136.4	....Savannah Farm..	68.5	10 55			
		...	137.0	.......Wetmore...	68.0	...			
	6	3 55	139.5	.....Cambria...... ♂	65.4	10 45	5		
	A. M.	4 10	144.2	......Grady....	60.7	10 34	P. M.		
	†6 00	4 21	150.3	..Tellico Junc.³.♂	54.6	10 19	8 08		
	6 41	4 15	160.1	...Madisonville... ♂	44.8	9 55	7 28		
	7 06	5 00	165.6	.....Brakeville....	39.3	9 40	6 58		
	7 31	5 15	170.9	......McGhees..... ♂	34.0	9 25	6 33		
	7 43	5 26	174.1	......Alleghany... ♂	30.8	9 13	6 18		
	8 03	5 42	181.5	.......Kisers...... ♂	23.4	8 57	5 58		
	8 11	5 48	183.5	....Friendsville... ♂	21.4	8 51	5 48		
	8 36	6 04	190.2	.... Louisville.... ♂	14.7	8 36	5 25		
	9 01	6 20	197.1	.....Singleton.....	7.8	8 20	4 56		
	9 25		202.9	.Bridge Junction¹	2.0	8 03	4 30		
	9 30	6 10	204.9	..... Knoxville⁴...	0	*8 00	†4 25		
	A.M.	P.M.		ARRIVE] [LEAVE		A.M.	P.M.		
		P. M.		LEAVE] [ARRIVE		A.M.			
		*2 00	0	...Blue Ridge.	25.5	12 20			
		2 22	5.5	...Mineral Bluff...	20.0	12 03			
		2 50	12.5	......State Line.....	13.0	11 30			
		3 05	14.5	..... Culberson	11.0	11 20			
		3 22	18.5	.......Notla.... ♂	7.0	11 00			
		3 50	25.5	.....Murphy⁵.....	0	*1030			
		P.M.		ARRIVE] [LEAVE		A.M.			

CONNECTIONS.—¹With Western & Atlantic R.R. ²With Nash. & Tellico Ry. ³With Knoxville & Augusta R.R. ⁴With East Tennessee, Va. & Georgia Ry. System; Knoxville, Cumberland Gap & Louisville Ry. ⁵With Murphy Branch Richmond and Danville R.R.

The 1893 *Official Railway Guide* lists two trains a day between Atlanta, Georgia, and Murphy, North Carolina. There, a connection could be made with the Southern Railway.

— 123 —

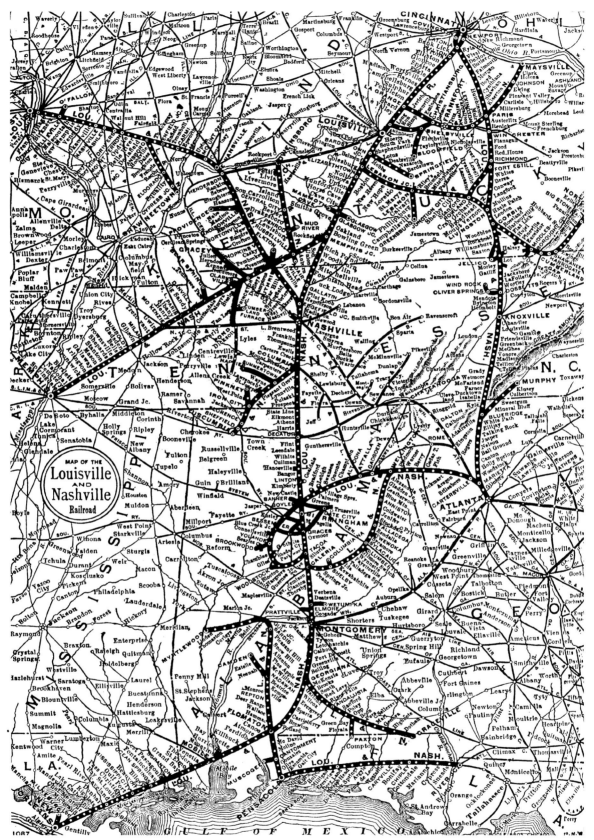

During the Asheville, North Carolina, flood of 1916, this was the only route of four to survive the damage and allow relief supplies to be carried to the stricken area. The supplies started in Atlanta, Georgia, turned northeast on the L&N Murphy Branch, interchanged with the Southern, and were then brought on into Asheville. Courtesy of *The Official Railway Guide*.

The L&N Murphy Branch local is photographed at Blue Ridge, Georgia, on July 28, 1968. Photograph by O.W. Kimsey. Collection of Frank Ardrey.

Georgia Northeastern Railroad #8704 leads two other units south out of Tate, Georgia, on December 11, 1992. The first two units are GP-18s built in 1960 for the Nickle Plate Railroad and later acquired by the Georgia Northeastern Railroad. Photograph by Cary F. Poole.

L&N #4000, a GP-38, pulls a string of empty log cars across a trestle near Ranger, North Carolina, on March 10, 1980. The L&N abandoned the connection between Murphy, North Carolina, and Blue Ridge, Georgia, just a few years later. Photograph by Jim King.

supplies to the Western North Carolina area. Supplies were brought northwest from Atlanta to Marietta on the former Western and Atlanta Railroad. Then the supplies were sent north on the former Atlanta, Knoxville & Northern Railroad to Blue Ridge, Georgia. There the supplies were headed northeast on the former Marietta & North Georgia line to Murphy. At Murphy the line interchanged with the Southern Railway, and the supplies were brought east to the devastated town of Asheville.

This rerouting of supplies continued for several months as the other three lines into Asheville were being rebuilt. It was reported that the line handled an extremely large volume of traffic during this time and was due much needed repair after the Southern lines to Asheville were restored.

The line continued until 1980, when flooding caused severe damage to portions of the line from Blue Ridge, Georgia, to Murphy, North Carolina. In 1982 the L&N petitioned the Interstate Commerce Commission to abandon that portion of the line. After much local protest, the ICC consented to the abandonment.

As of 1994, the portion of the line from Marietta to Blue Ridge is still operated by the Georgia Northeastern Railroad. This line is based out of Tate, Georgia, with its main connection with the CSX Transportation at Elizabeth (Marietta), Georgia. The line terminates a couple of miles from the Glover Manufacturing Company. The company was founded by J. B. Glover, the man responsible for holding the Marietta & North Georgia Railroad together in its financially troubled early days.

The Georgia Northeastern Railroad operates 68 miles of track between Marietta and Ellijay. Current motive power is furnished by first generation diesel locomotives, namely GP-9s and GP-18s.

CSX operates the remaining section between Copperhill, Tennessee, and Blue Ridge, Georgia, on a once-a-week basis. Negotiations are currently being held to lease this operation to the Georgia Northeastern Railroad as well, thereby giving the short line a second division.

CLIFFSIDE RAILROAD

"They built a mill, added a town—and tied them to the world beyond with 3.68 miles of well scrubbed railroad."

—H. Reid

With a sense of humor, H. Reid, noted railroad historian and researcher, described in one sentence the history, length, and purpose of the Cliffside Railroad.

The original concept was to construct a mill, and ship raw materials in and finished gingham cloth out by mule-drawn wagons. As expected with a successful venture, the wagons could not keep up with the required delivery schedule, and plans were soon developed to construct a railroad.

LEGEND
— Cliffside Railroad

MAP OF THE
CLIFFSIDE RAILROAD

The Cliffside Railroad is illustrated with its proximity to the major railroads located in the area, including the Southern, Clinchfield, Seaboard Air Line, and various other smaller railroads. Courtesy of *The Official Railway Guide*.

The plan took into consideration that the Seaboard Air Line Railroad came within three miles of the mill, and negotiations turned to that railroad to construct a spur into the mill complex. After some negotiations, a contract was agreed upon and the location of the interchange point would be referred to as Cliffside Junction. The arrangement with the Seaboard Air Line Railroad was to include rails for the three miles into the mill complex and ample sidings within the complex itself. These sidings would serve five mills.

CLIFFSIDE RAILROAD COMPANY.
R. R. HAYNES, President, Cliffside, N.C.
Trains leave Cliffside, N.C., for **Cliffside Junction**[1], N.C. (3 miles), †6 55, †8 20 a.m., †12 45 noon, †3 45, *5 30 p.m. Returning, leave Cliffside Junction †7 05, †8 30 a.m., †12 55 noon, †4 00, †5 40 p.m. Additional train service on Sundays. *January*, 1915.
* Daily; † daily, except Sunday.
Connection.—[1] With Seaboard Air Line Ry. *Eastern time.*

The Cliffside Railroad Company was owned and operated by Cone Mills. The connection was with the Seaboard Air Line Railroad at Cliffside Junction, a distance of three miles. Courtesy of *The Official Railway Guide*.

The first three locomotives purchased by the Cliffside Railroad were secondhand 0-4-4 Forneys which once operated on the elevated railroads of New York City. Collection of Tom L. Sink.

Grading for the railroad began in 1903, and the railroad was formally chartered by North Carolina in 1905.

The Cliffside Railroad was noted for the variety of its motive power during the course of its corporate history. The first three locomotives on the line were secondhand 15-ton Forney locomotives in a 0-4-4 wheel configuration. The locomotives had previously served on the elevated railroads of New York City.

The Cliffside also purchased two Glover Machine

ANNUAL LOCOMOTIVE BOILER INSPECTION AND REPAIR REPORT.

Nashville, Chattanooga & St. Louis Ry. Co.

LOCOMOTIVE { NUMBER / INITIAL }

In accordance with the Act of Congress, approved February 17, 1911, and the rules and instructions issued in pursuance thereof and approved by the Interstate Commerce Commission, I hereby certify that on _____, 1923 at _____, I inspected the boiler of Locomotive No. _____ and the appurtenances thereof, operated by the NASHVILLE, CHATTANOOGA & ST. LOUIS RY. COMPANY; that all defects disclosed by said inspection have been repaired, except as noted on the back of this report; that to the best of my knowledge and belief said boiler and appurtenances thereof are in a proper condition for use, and safe to operate with a steam pressure of _____ pounds per square inch.

1. Date of previous hydrostatic test
2. Date of previous removal of flues
3. Date of previous removal of lagging from barrel
4. Date of previous removal of caps from flexible stay bolts
5. Were all flues removed?
6. Number of flues removed
7. Was all lagging on firebox removed?
8. Was all lagging on barrel removed?
9. Were caps removed from all flexible stay bolts?
10. Were dome cap and throttle standpipe removed?
11. Hydrostatic test pressure of ____ pounds was applied.
12. Were both injectors tested and left in good condition?
13. Were steam gauges tested and left in good condition?
14. Safety valves set to pop at ___ pounds ___ pounds ___ pounds.
15. Was boiler washed; water glass cocks and gauge cocks cleaned?

16. Were all steam leaks repaired?
17. Number of broken crown stays and stay bolts renewed
18. Condition of exterior of barrel
19. Condition of interior of barrel
20. Condition of firebox sheets and flues
21. Condition of arch tubes
22. Condition of water-bar tubes
23. Condition of cross stays
24. Condition of throat stays
25. Condition of sling stays
26. Condition of crown bars, braces, and bolts
27. Condition of dome braces
28. Condition of back head braces
29. Condition of front flue sheet braces

I hereby certify that, to the best of my knowledge and belief the above report is correct.

STATE OF _____
COUNTY OF _____ } ss.
Subscribed and sworn to before me this ___ day of _____, 1923

_____ Inspector.
_____ Officer in Charge.
_____ Notary Public.

THIS REPORT NOT TO BE FOLDED)

The Glover Machine Works of Marietta, Georgia, cast or machined most of its parts for the locomotives it constructed. The boiler, however, was one of the few parts not built by the Glover plant. Above is the inspection form used to certify the boiler for the Cliffside 2-6-2 tank engine, which was to be numbered 18. Note the form was signed on a NC&StL (Nashville, Chattanooga & St. Louis) inspection form, but the corporate name was struck through and the Cliffside Railroad name was penned instead.

The number to the side of the inspection form, 131818, refers to the unique Glover manner of numbering its locomotives. The first four digits, 1318, refer to the cylinder dimensions of 13" × 18". The last 18 refers to the numerical sequence of construction; hence, the #18 was the eighteenth locomotive produced by Glover with 13" × 18" cylinders, and the number later stuck with the Cliffside Railroad, as the locomotive was referred to as the #18. Courtesy of the Glover Machine Works.

Works locomotives—one was a used locomotive, and the second was purchased new. The used locomotive was a 2-6-0 Mogul originally built for the West Bay Naval Stores and Lumber Company, then sold to the Southeastern Iron & Equipment Company, where it was purchased by the Cliffside Railroad in 1922.

A year later, the Cliffside Railroad went shopping for a secondhand locomotive but ended up purchasing a new Glover 2-6-2 side tank engine. The locomotive was one of the larger models which Glover produced during its locomotive construction period. The coal bunker could carry 1,500 pounds of fuel, and the two side-mounted tanks could carry 1,200 gallons of water. The locomotive was designated #18 and had a purchase price of $10,000.

A year after the locomotive was delivered in 1923, Glover Machine Works received a disturbing letter from R. R. Hayes, president of the Cliffside Railroad. In the letter, Hayes said the locomotive had failed to live up to its marketing promises and that the Cliffside Railroad was very disappointed in its performance. After much correspondence between Glover Machine Works in Marietta, Georgia, and Cliffside Railroad in North Carolina, Glover decided to send a mechanical engineer to the Cliffside Railroad to inspect the locomotive.

Upon arrival, the Glover mechanic discovered the Cliffside Railroad mechanics had drilled a larger hole on the steam dome to facilitate the mounting of a larger whistle. The filings from the drilling had fallen

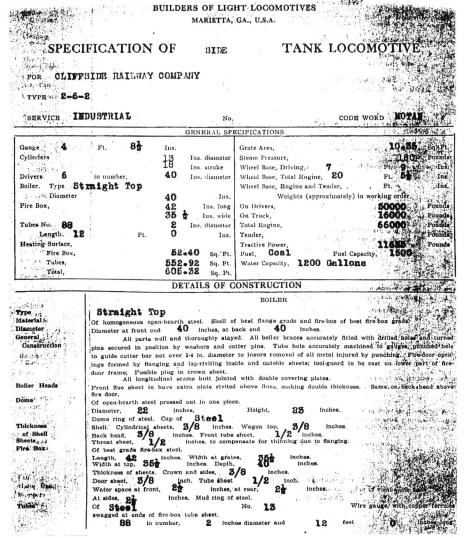

GLOVER MACHINE WORKS

BUILDERS OF LIGHT LOCOMOTIVES
MARIETTA, GA., U.S.A.

SPECIFICATION OF   SIDE   TANK LOCOMOTIVE

FOR   CLIFFSIDE RAILWAY COMPANY

TYPE   2-6-2

SERVICE   INDUSTRIAL   No,   CODE WORD   NOTAN

GENERAL SPECIFICATIONS

Gauge, 4 Ft. 8½ Ins.		Grate Area,	10.35 Sq.Ft.
Cylinders 13/18 Ins. diameter		Steam Pressure,	180 Pounds
Ins. stroke		Wheel Base, Driving, 7	Ft. 9 Ins.
Drivers 6 in number, 40 Ins. diameter		Wheel Base, Total Engine, 20	Ft. 5 Ins.
Boiler. Type Straight Top		Wheel Base, Engine and Tender,	Ft. Ins.
Diameter 40 Ins.		Weights (approximately) in working order	
Fire Box, 42 Ins. long		On Drivers,	50000 Pounds
35¼ Ins. wide		On Truck,	16000 Pounds
Tubes. No. 88 2 Ins. diameter		Total Engine,	66000 Pounds
Length. 12 Ft. 0 Ins.		Tender,	Pounds
Heating Surface,		Tractive Power,	11685 Pounds
Fire Box, 52.40 Sq. Ft.		Fuel, Coal Fuel Capacity, 1500	
Tubes, 552.92 Sq. Ft.		Water Capacity, 1200 Gallons	
Total, 605.32 Sq. Ft.			

DETAILS OF CONSTRUCTION

BOILER

Straight Top

Type / Material / Diameter / General Construction: Of homogeneous open-hearth steel. Shell of best flange grade and fire-box of best fire box grade. Diameter at front end 40 inches, at back end 40 inches.

All parts well and thoroughly stayed. All boiler braces accurately fitted with drilled holes and turned pins secured in position by washers and cotter pins. Tube hole accurately machined to gauges, punched hole to guide cutter bar not over 3-4 in. diameter to insure removal of all metal injured by punching. Fire-door openings formed by flanging and lap-riviting inside and outside sheets; tool-guard to be cast on lower part of fire-door frame; Fusible plug in crown sheet.

All longitudinal seams butt jointed with double covering plates.

Boiler Heads — Front flue sheet to have extra plate rivited above flues, making double thickness. Same on back head above fire door.

Dome — Of open-hearth steel pressed out in one piece.
Diameter, 22 inches,   Height, 23 inches.
Dome ring of steel. Cap of **Steel**

Thickness of Shell Sheets — Shell. Cylindrical sheets, 3/8 inches. Wagon top, 3/8 inches.
Back head, 3/8 inches. Front tube sheet, 1/2 inches.
Throat sheet, 1/2 inches, to compensate for thinning due to flanging.

Fire Box — Of best grade fire-box steel.
Length, 42 inches. Width at grates, 35¼ inches.
Width at top, 35¼ inches. Depth, 40 inches.
Thickness of sheets. Crown and sides, 3/8 inches.
Door sheet, 3/8 inch. Tube sheet, 1/2 inch.
Water space at front, 2½ inches, at rear, 2½ inches.
At sides, 2½ inches. Mud ring of steel. No. 13
Of **Steel** swagged at ends of fire-box tube sheet.

Tubes — 88 in number, 2 inches diameter and 12 feet 0 inches long. Wire gauge, with copper ferrules.

The Cliffside Railroad placed an order for a new locomotive through the Glover Machine Works in 1923. The form above was used to draw up the specifications for the Cliffside's new 2-6-2 side tank locomotive. The locomotive was to be used for switching duties at the Cliffside mill and would come equipped with a cowcatcher on the front and rear. The side mounted water tanks were to be used in lieu of a trailing tender. Each of the two had a capacity of 600 gallons of water. Fuel capacity was 1,500 pounds of coal and was carried in a compartment behind the cab. Courtesy of the Glover Machine Works.

into the throttle linkage and had prevented the engineer from being able to completely open or close the throttle. The Cliffside mechanics could not find the problem, and the locomotive engineers worsened the problem by the method they used to halt the locomotive. Since they could not fully stop the locomotive by closing the throttle, the engineers would throw the engine into reverse, momentarily halting the locomotive. At this split second of halting, the engineer would lock down the brakes. After performing this maneuver hundreds of times, the entire linkage had become stretched.

A battle soon ensued between the Glover Machine Works and the Cliffside Railroad over who should pay for the inspection trip and the salary of the mechanic while on Cliffside's property. Through correspondence between both parties, the bill went unpaid but hotly contested. The issue was finally settled when the Cliffside Railroad needed spare parts for the #18 and found the Glover Machine Works to be the only source for the parts. With the new order for the spare parts also came payment for the inspection trip a year before.

Another fairly unusual locomotive the Cliffside Railroad had in service was a Vulcan-built engine numbered 110. The engine had originally been designed as a wood burner but was converted to coal fuel for use on the Cliffside Railroad.

The Cliffside Railroad did not dieselize until its purchase of a GE-built 35-ton locomotive. This diesel made its first run on July 23, 1962, after the #40 was retired earlier that month. The #110 was retired in August 1963. The small diesel locomotive was sold back to the Birmingham Rail & Locomotive Company in 1970. In 1968, due to increased freight business, a larger and more powerful engine had been purchased, a GE-built 70-tonner.

The Cliffside Railroad held on until the late 1980s, when it ceased operations. The #113, the 70-tonner, is still on the premises in the engine shed, awaiting its final fate or better days. Most of the rails remain intact, but the freight is now sent out by tractor-trailers.

Cliffside #18 is photographed in Cliffside, North Carolina, during April 1939. Most of the lettering on the locomotive has long since faded. Collection of Harold K. Vollrath.

The #13 was the largest diesel-electric to serve the Cliffside Railroad. It was purchased in 1968 and remains on the premises as of 1993, even though the rails are unused. Photograph by Tom L. Sink.

Cliffside #108, taken July 2, 1941, is a Baldwin 2-6-2 Prairie which formerly belonged to the Ingham-Burnett Lumber Company. Collection of Tom King.

The #110 pulls two boxcars as the brakeman rides on the front pilot. Collection of Tom L. Sink.

Coupled ahead of the #110 is the Cliffside Railroad's combination baggage and caboose car. Collection of Tom L. Sink.

This small 35-ton GE locomotive forced the retirement of the Cliffside's last two steam-powered locomotives, the #40 and #110. Collection of Mac Connery.

Cliffside #40 is a 2-8-0 which was obtained from the Lancaster & Chester Railroad in 1947. The locomotive was sold to the New Hope & Ivyland Railroad in Pennsylvania in 1962. The engine was built by Baldwin in 1925 as their #58824. Collection of Tom L. Sink.

A General Electric 44-tonner, the Cliffside #20 is photographed in Cliffside, North Carolina, in November 1963. Collection of Harold K. Vollrath.

GLOVER MACHINE WORKS
Marietta, Georgia

The Glover family has had a long and interesting history in not only the railroad and related fields, but as a general manufacturer as well. In addition, the Glover Machine Works represents one of the few "Southern" locomotive builders.

The family moved from South Carolina to Georgia in 1848, and four years later the patriarch, John Heyward Glover, was elected mayor of Marietta, Georgia. The first venture into business was a tannery, which operated until its destruction by Union forces in 1863. After the Civil War, the family purchased the Withers' Iron Foundry, which they have operated until current times.

The iron foundry had a long association with the logging and mining industries, including the manufacture of upright boiler-equipped steam log skidders. The company even went as far as drafting the plans for a steam-powered derrick, but the prototype was never constructed.

In 1902 Glover's first steam locomotive on record was constructed. This locomotive was a 3' gauge 0-4-0T and was purchased by a brick company in Macon, Georgia.

Over the next 28 years, the company produced 191 locomotives, which were shipped across the southeastern United States. Some new locomotives made their way as far as California and Washington and several foreign countries. One locomotive reportedly went to Russia.

The last locomotive on record also went to a brick company and was of the same identical wheel configuration as the very first locomotive, a 0-4-0T. After this locomotive left the plant on April 19, 1930, all locomotive construction ceased.

The majority of Glover locomotives were utilized in the Southeast in the logging, naval stores, and mining/quarry industries. A small number of the lo-

Inside the Glover Machine Works, September 1904. The overhead crane lifts a narrow gauge 0-4-0 onto a standard gauge flatcar for shipment. Photograph by Glover Machine Works. Collection of Dick Hillman.

Builder's photograph of a 2-6-0 originally purchased by the West Bay Naval Stores and Lumber Company. The locomotive was later rebuilt and became Cliffside #26. Photograph by Glover Machine Works. Courtesy of Dick Hillman.

A 3/4 view builder's photograph of the Cliffside #18, a 2-6-2T. Photograph by Glover Machine Works. Courtesy of Dick Hillman.

Cliffside #26 was a 2-6-0 Mogul built by the Glover Machine Works of Marietta, Georgia. The locomotive was purchased used from the Southern Iron & Equipment Company in 1922 and was scrapped in 1938. Collection of Mac Connery.

A builder's side view of Cliffside #18. The locomotive was built new for the Cliffside Railroad in 1923. Photograph by Glover Machine Works. Courtesy of Dick Hillman.

comotives did wind up on common carrier railroads. The company was often mistakenly identified as a manufacturer of only narrow gauge locomotives. Review of the company records clearly demonstrates that 56% of the 191 locomotives constructed were standard gauge.

The Glover archives are currently intact and offer a fascinating window into the rise and fall of the lumber industry in the United States. With the heavy influx of orders from logging companies in the teens and early twenties, the company experienced a boom in locomotive construction. However, with the approach of the late 1920s, orders fell off and the company experienced a high degree of difficulty in collecting payment for engines and replacement parts.

The company survives today as a manufacturer of high-pressure steam fittings for the oil business. The Glover Machine Works has an excellent reputation for the quality of its work and reportedly has never had a fitting fail in the field. It is the oldest family-owned business in Georgia.

(This information was provided courtesy of Dick Hillman, director of marketing for the Georgia Northeastern Railroad. Mr. Hillman has extensively researched the Glover Machine Works.)

THE LAWNDALE RAILWAY & INDUSTRIAL COMPANY

In 1875 an ex-Confederate major, H. F. Schenck, built a cotton mill on Knob Creek. The mill was named Schenck's Factory and was located ten miles north of Cleveland County's seat of Shelby.

A second mill was erected in 1888 two miles south of the original factory after a partnership with James E. Reynolds was formed. This second mill was named Cleveland Cotton Mill, and the small community which sprang up around the mill became known as Lawndale.

After ten years of hauling freight by wagons to the nearest railhead, the company had other ventures in mind. At that time, the plants relied solely on water power to supply the needs of the cotton mills. After much discussion, it was decided to experiment with either coal or electric power, whichever was cheaper, to supply power to the plants.

The discussion centered on the knowledge that whether the mills were fired by coal or supplied with electricity produced by coal, only a rail line could bring in sufficient quantities of the fuel to handle the needs.

It was announced on February 24, 1899, in *The Manufacturer's Record* that a railroad from Shelby to Lawndale would be built. This was a family decision, since James Schenck's son John, an attorney, agreed to help run the family business.

In March 1899 the gauge was finally decided upon. At first, indicators pointed toward a standard gauge line. However, in the end the decision was to build the line in a 3' gauge. When questioned about the decision, the elder Schenck responded, "By doggies, I don't want my freight cars traveling all over the country."

The actual construction was commenced on May 10, 1899. The construction of the rail line was relatively easy considering past construction problems encountered in Western North Carolina. Very little

The #4 pulls a short train to Lawndale Junction. The brakeman rides atop the boxcar and sets the brakes when necessary as the train rolls down a slight grade. Collection of Doug Walker.

fill needed to be placed due to the gently rolling countryside which the construction followed. The ballast consisted primarily of dirt with a few cinders.

Initially the line was laid in 25-pound rail, but it was upgraded to 40-pound rail in 1907. Eight miles of track were laid, and when the line was completed on November 11, 1899, only $49,000 had been spent. Two miles of dual trackage on the Southern Railway accounted for the first of the track and connected the Lawndale in Shelby with the Seaboard Air Line Railroad.

The initial fleet of rolling stock arrived from the nearby Chester and Lenoir Narrow Gauge Railroad.

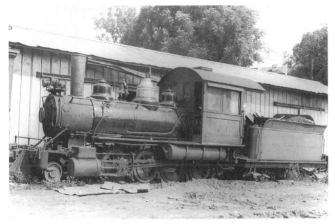

Lawndale #4 was a Vulcan-built 2-8-0 constructed in 1908. It was equipped with two small headlights after the customary single headlight was destroyed in an accident. The engine was scrapped in 1945. Collection of Tom L. Sink.

Lawndale #4 pulls a southbound train from Lawndale to Lawndale Junction. The scene was captured by R.W. Richardson near Double Shoals in March 1942. Collection of Frank Moore.

The Lawndale #5 is shown outside the engine house located at Lawndale, North Carolina. The #5 was a Vulcan-built 2-8-0 Consolidation, much like its sister unit, the #4. The #4 can be seen in the right bay with its distinctive dual headlights. Collection of Doug Walker.

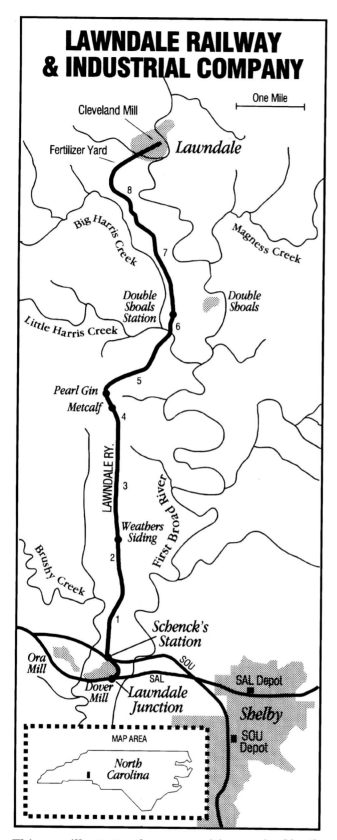

LAWNDALE RAILWAY & INDUSTRIAL COMPANY

One Mile

Cleveland Mill

Fertilizer Yard

Lawndale

8

Big Harris Creek

Magness Creek

7

Double Shoals Station

Double Shoals

Little Harris Creek

6

5

Pearl Gin Metcalf

4

LAWNDALE RY.

3

First Broad River

Weathers Siding

2

Brushy Creek

1

Schenck's Station

Ora Mill

SOU

Dover Mill

SAL

SAL Depot

Lawndale Junction

Shelby

SOU Depot

MAP AREA

North Carolina

This map illustrates the communities serviced by the Lawndale Railway and the connections with the Southern Railway and the Seaboard Air Line Railroad. Courtesy of Chris Ford.

The Chester and Lenoir had been sold in 1897 with the intention to standard gauge the line. With this in mind, the narrow gauge rolling stock was not needed and was disposed of to the Lawndale Railway.

From 1902 until 1906, the Lawndale experienced a brief but unusual business upswing. A stroke of luck occurred when monazite was discovered in Cleveland County. At the time, gas was widely utilized for lighting, and the gas lamps had mantles made from processed monazite, which glowed brightly when lit. As it happened, this rare material is found only in about a half-dozen locations in the world. Brazil was the most prolific producer, but the trade was largely controlled by a German-held monopoly. When this corporation doubled the price, suppliers were forced to excavate and process the material elsewhere. For a brief period, the Lawndale enjoyed a burst of activity. A magnetic separator was even constructed in Shelby in 1905 to facilitate refinement.

It must be noted that only 3,000 tons of monazite was a general rule for a year's supply for the entire world. The actual business spurt came from side-related traffic, such as bringing in mining supplies for the miners and the camps. The boom came to an abrupt halt in 1906 when the German monopoly suddenly lowered its price by 50%. This made the American-mined monazite too expensive to compete with the Brazilian ore, and operations soon ceased in Cleveland County.

As with most successful rail operations, the Lawndale survived the monazite crash with a more stable increase in traffic relating to the cotton mills. The mills at Knob Creek and Lawndale had increased ca-

Vulcan-built #5 is at work in Lawndale, North Carolina, in October 1940. Collection of Harold K. Vollrath.

pacity, and new mills were being put on line. The general daily pattern was for ginned cotton to go north to the mills and finished yarn and thread to be sent south to Shelby.

Over most of its corporate history, the Lawndale earned money for its parent company. However, the railroad began seriously considering shutting down during the early 1940s and turning transportation over to trucks. Even though the railroad was still profitable, considerable revenue was being lost to highway traffic.

In April of 1943, the last train made its run, even though the last official run had taken place on December 31, 1941. The ICC approved abandonment, and a salvage firm began the job of recovering the track and rolling stock for their scrap value. By 1945, little remained of the railroad.

The Lawndale #5, along with the combination coach and caboose car, pulls a single boxcar. Collection of Doug Walker.

LOGGING IN WESTERN NORTH CAROLINA

The valleys, hills, and mountains of Western North Carolina contained huge unspoiled virgin stands of timber and natural resources before the 1880s. Natural resources targeted for exploitation starting in the latter part of the nineteenth century included those vast timber reserves. One early observer was so impressed by the expanse of the forests that he labeled the Great Smoky Mountains area as "a wilderness of the deepest green."

The history of logging in the area can generally be classified into two distinct periods. The first, extending from approximately 1880 until 1900, is referred to as either the selective or peripheral cutting period. For this type of logging, only selected species were desired and the loggers operated only in areas of easy access.

The first species sought were black walnut, ash, and cherry; and later, poplar and oak were sought. It was generally considered inefficient and economically unfeasible for selective cutting to supply large mills with the amount of timber needed to keep them operating. The opening of the Murphy Branch of the Southern Railway in the 1890s proved a boom to a new type of logging—clear-cutting.

With the coming of steel rails to Western North Carolina, logging expanded on a grand scale. By 1914, over 200 miles of logging rails operated in this portion of the state. Most large timber companies began purchasing huge tracts of land in the rush to establish their territories and to stake out a connection along the tracks of the Southern Railway.

A second boom occurred when the Champion Fibre Company at Canton, North Carolina, was completed. This plant furnished a market for wood by-products which normally would not have provided a profit for sawmills. This new market not only benefited the large operations, but also the small, family-owned mills.

And while the logging industry experienced an evolution from selective cutting to large-scale cutting, the industry experienced a revolution as well in the

A W.M. Ritter American log loader in Swain County, North Carolina, at work near Proctor on Hazel Creek. The photograph was taken in 1917. Courtesy of the Austin-Brooks Collection, Ramsey Library, UNC-Asheville.

methods of log removal. One of the first methods employed to move logs to the mill was the splash dam. One such practice was observed on Hazel Creek, above Tuckasegee. In this method, the loggers rolled or "ballhooted" logs down cleared paths into large streams. Meanwhile, the creek had been dammed upstream in order to back up the water level. After a sufficient number of logs had been gathered in the stream below, the water would be released either by a control gate or the dynamiting of the entire dam. The rush of water would hopefully carry the logs down to the mill itself or to another dam, where the process would then be repeated. The practice was not very popular due to the number of logs which would be lost in the rush downstream.

The next method employed was the practice of laying pole or tram roads for the removal of timber. The tram road resembled in some sense a railroad, with one major exception: the rails were made of logs. The practice was to lay poles of nine to twelve inches in diameter in which the butts all pointed in one direction. The top of one pole was lap-jointed to the butt of the following pole. This wooden "rail" was then held in place by wooden stakes driven into the ground.

The earliest means of removing logs was the tram road. The wide-flanged cars rolled over rails made of stripped logs. Mules, horses, or oxen then removed the logs over the wooden rails from the area being harvested. Courtesy of the U.S. Forest Service.

The method of propulsion was draft animals, except on some down grades where gravity was employed. Most tram roads did not exceed more than a couple of miles in length. In order to achieve stability, most tram roads had a fairly wide gauge, generally of five to six feet in width. Due to the fact that draft animals were employed, tram roads seldom exceeded 1.5% grades. As might be expected, due to irregularity of the poles serving as rails, the flanges on the log cars were oversized. In a few cases, geared locomotives were equipped with the same over-sized flanged wheels in order to move timber.

In 1876 a Michigan logger, Scott Garrish, proved steel rails could be employed to remove timber and deliver it to the local mill. Soon, loggers across the nation, and particularly in Western North Carolina, employed a variety of gauges using steel rail for timber removal.

Several strong advantages swayed the loggers to adopt the new technology. The first of many advantages was that rails, by facilitating heavier equipment, opened up areas for logging which had previously remained inaccessible. Second, unlike splash dams, railroads lost no logs in the transportation to the mill. When loggers depended upon splash dams for moving logs, a certain percentage was always expected to be lost. Third, loggers could haul out every species of tree, including hardwoods. This increased the stand-per-acre count and contributed to the overall profitability of the operation.

A different method of rail utilization was soon adopted in Western North Carolina in order to reach timber reserves inaccessible to normal locomotives. This new method employed inclined railroads, on which loaded and empty cars were drawn up and over mountains by cables. The machinery used to raise and lower the cars in Western North Carolina was generally a stationary steam engine located at the mountain crest. Some referred to these engines as "donkey engines." The tracks were laid over the side of the slope which needed to be scaled. Most inclines, while navigating extreme grades, generally were laid in a straight line down the face of the grade. Inclines built on curved grades suffered from two handicaps. First, additional drag was encountered, and this required additional horsepower to be overcome. Second, an incline on a curve needed rollers to keep the cables centered between the rails. These rollers drastically reduced the life of the cable due to the constant friction.

The Champion operation which ran between Canton and Sunburst had an incline which the company referred to as the "mile and a half run."

Inclined railroads were used to lower cars down steep slopes in Western North Carolina. This incline was estimated at a 50% grade. Courtesy of the U.S. Forest Service.

As might be expected, the safety of inclines raised many concerns, and the crews had to be ever vigilant for runaway cars and frayed cables. The obvious advantage to inclined railroads was the ability to tap timber resources previously inaccessible to standard railroads. The con to the inclines was the inherent danger of lowering loaded log cars down mountain-

sides. Even with the danger, the practice enjoyed moderate success in the area, particularly when logs could be moved down the mountainside by inclines, then loaded onto standard railcars at the bottom of the inclines.

A decision often faced by loggers involved what type of motive power to employ on a logging railroad. However, before 1880 rod locomotives were the only type available.

Rod locomotives are the type in which power is transmitted from the cylinders to the driving wheels by a connecting rod. While the locomotives gave a gentler ride and greater speed capacity than later types, they were not totally practical for logging purposes. The rigid frame prevented a rod engine from being able to handle tight curves.

A logger finally answered the industry prayer in the late 1870s, when Ephram Shay of Michigan designed a gear-driven locomotive. The major difference between a rod and geared locomotive was the manner in which the power was delivered to the driving wheels. The geared locomotive delivered power to

An overturned Shay in Swain County, North Carolina, in 1917. Log loader #2 and another Shay help with the recovery efforts. Courtesy of the Austin-Brooks Collection, Ramsey Library, UNC-Asheville.

every wheel through the use of drive shafts running to every truck. This permitted a geared locomotive to use lighter rail, lighter bridges, and poorer track, and at the same time climb steeper grades.

The major negative characteristic of a geared locomotive was the sacrifice in speed. Top speed for some geared locomotives was 12 miles per hour, and most could not deliver that speed on an extended basis. However, since logs were a non-perishable commodity, the sacrifice of speed was not viewed by most loggers as a handicap.

Two types of geared locomotives were soon on the market. The most popular was the side-mounted cylinders model perfected by Shay. This model was named after the inventor and was built by the Lima Locomotive Works of Lima, Ohio. A similar model was constructed on the west coast by the Willamette Company of Oregon.

The center shaft variety was marketed by two major companies, the Heisler and the Climax companies. Both employed an articulated shaft placed under the boiler. This shaft transmited power to the front and rear trucks by joining with pinions which in turn meshed into gears on each axle.

A selling point for loggers on geared locomotives was the ease of maintenance. Since the gears on this type of locomotive were exposed, most camp blacksmiths soon learned to service the machines in the field. A geared locomotive was sent to the shops only when immediate repairs could not be completed by the local mechanics.

The economic impact of logging in Western North Carolina cannot be underestimated. The sheer number of employed loggers, train crews, sawmill hands, and people of various other trades helped to open up the area. It may be added that many of the techniques practiced by early loggers left the mountain scarred and denuded of any vegetation. And while these practices, based largely on ignorance, cannot be ignored, the overall impact of logging on the region was apparent.

The employment was of such a grand scale that workers were recruited to fill the vacant jobs. The Black Mountain Railroad and the Clinchfield Railroad employed Italian, Australian, and Irish immigrant workers. The Tennessee & North Carolina Railroad out of Newport, Tennessee, hired Native Americans from the Cherokee tribe to serve on its section crews. The Sunburst operation of Champion Fibre Company was so extensive that it had its own school system, which at that time included a separate school for the children of the black mill workers.

The mills at one time supported communities which were quite extensive for the period. Each contributed to the economic development of the area; but even more importantly, each helped to open an isolated and economically undeveloped area of North Carolina. The list of now defunct mills and associated railroads is a long, proud list. To mention a few would be to include the W. M. Ritter operation with its several locations; the Carr, Glouchester, and Moltz operations of Transylvania County; the Blackwood Brothers; the Laurel River Company; Craggy Lumber; and Perley & Crockett Lumber. It is difficult at best to imagine some of the operations at their heyday when they employed hundreds within the plant and supported communities of even more hundreds in the surrounding areas.

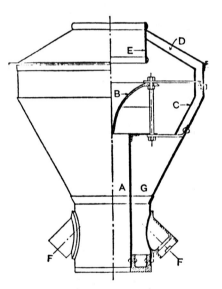

In Western North Carolina, the earliest rail logging operations employed wood-burning locomotives. One of the problems encountered with this type of fuel was the consequence of possible forest fires. To remedy this problem, various spark arresters were developed to prevent sparks from flying from the stack. One such device was the Radley-Hunter Spark Arrester. This model was employed on a widespread basis throughout the region. The device allowed smoke and cinders to pass through the smoke chamber and (A) then strike a spiral cone. This (B) caused the smoke and cinders to swirl, and large cinders were pushed outward by centrifugal force, against the perforated screen plate (C). The plate had openings large enough to permit the passage of cinders into the spark chamber (D). The fine mesh screen (E) contained the live sparks. Once through this screen, the weight of the cinders caused them to fall into the waiting receptacle (G). The cinders were then removed through the cleaning-out holes (F).
This type of device allowed the capture of the larger, more dangerous ignited sparks and thus prevented them from escaping the stack. The smaller, less harmful sparks were allowed to escape the stack altogether. Courtesy of the U.S. Department of Agriculture.

The scene above represents the most common method of loading logs for delivery to the mill. Logs were (1) "yarded" by means of an upright stationary steam engine, sometimes referred to as a steam donkey. The steam engine pulled a string of logs, which had been chained one to another. After being yarded, a second steam engine (2) used pulleys to lift and load the logs onto log cars. After loading, the train (3) headed to the mill, where the logs were cut into lumber. From the mill, the lumber was loaded onto flatcars or boxcars for delivery to market. Drawing by Anthony McCaleb.

A list of mills also should include those who have adapted and survived into modern times and continue to contribute to the economic base of the region. Bemis is a true survivor in every sense of the word, but Champion Paper in Canton, North Carolina, is probably the all-time winner in longevity. Originally on-line for production in 1908, the mill still employs thousands and remains a primary customer for the Norfolk Southern Railroad.

The original Canton, North Carolina, station, circa 1910-1915. The photograph was taken not long after the station opened. Collection of Jim King.

The Champion Fibre #71 is photographed in the Canton, North Carolina, yard. Craig Allen, second from the left, retired at the mandatory age of 65 with 52 years of service. He was employed at the age of 13 to carry water to men working on the construction of the Canton mill. Collection of Norma Fisher. Courtesy of the Canton Area Historical Museum.

A Champion Fibre locomotive is photographed in the wood yard, circa 1915. The crew, left to right, are Joe Childers, Craig Allen, Moody Howard, and an unknown crewman. Collection of Norma Fisher. Courtesy of the Canton Area Historical Museum.

Champion Fibre #21 is a 2-8-0 Consolidation. The crew poses for their photograph in the Canton, North Carolina, yard. Courtesy of the Canton Area Historical Museum.

MOUNT MITCHELL RAILROAD

Climax #8 with a steam log loader operating on the Perley & Crockett Lumber Company tracks in 1910. Courtesy of the Presbyterian Historical Foundation.

The Dickey & Campbell Company, one of the largest lumber producers in Western North Carolina, began construction of a narrow gauge line in 1911. The line originated at Black Mountain City and trav-

Camp Alice, near the summit of Mount Mitchell, was used as a base of operations for the timber removal, circa 1920. Courtesy of the Barnhill Collection, Pack Memorial Library, Asheville, North Carolina.

eled over 21 miles of track, some at grades over 5.25%. It included nine switchbacks and extremely sharp curves to facilitate the climb up Mount Mitchell.

On November 17, 1913, the disclosure was made of the sale of the Dickey & Campbell Lumber Company to the Perley & Crockett Company of Williamsburg, Pennsylvania. The sale included the band mill, which was to be increased to handle 110,000 board feet per day.

The new Perley & Crockett interests invested $1 million in developing their mill and transportation system. The timber reserves included 300,000,000 board feet, with spruce and balsam being two of the primary targets for removal. It was estimated in 1913 that 15 more years of timber cutting could be forecast. By 1914 the line had reached Camp Alice, near the summit of Mount Mitchell. This camp served as a base of operations for the removal of timber on the steep slopes of the mountain.

Perley & Crockett operations on Mt. Mitchell employed a couple of American log loaders, #9 being the front loader. A Climax locomotive is pushing the train upgrade. Collection of Red Haney.

The 1916 *Southern Lumberman* recalled a typical excursion to the summit of Mount Mitchell by a group of timbermen. The gentlemen who took the trip remarked on the extremely rugged terrain the line traveled through. The line traveled from Black Mountain, at the 3,000' elevation point, to within a few hundred feet of the summit of Mount Mitchell, which is listed by the U.S. Geologic Survey at 6,711'.

A procedure the loggers witnessed was the operation of an overhead skidder. This particular skidder pulled spruce logs up the side of the mountain utilizing a span of cable 2,200' in length.

Upon reaching Black Mountain on the return trip,

Tourists look over the side of Mount Mitchell after their journey to the summit. The photograph also depicts the complete deforestation due to the logging activities. Courtesy of the Barnhill Collection, Pack Memorial Library, Asheville, North Carolina.

An early postcard printed by the Southern Postcard Company of Asheville illustrates the third rail system employed at Ridgecrest on the Southern Railway tracks for the Mt. Mitchell Railroad. Collection of Doug Walker.

The scene above is identical to the scene below but has been "doctored" to be used as a postcard. The freight car has been painted to resemble a coach, and the brakemen have been removed. Courtesy of the Presbyterian Historical Foundation. Collection of Cary F. Poole.

The photograph above shows a Climax locomotive sandwiched between a string of coaches and a single open-sided freight car. Note the brakemen on the roofs of the freight car and the coaches. Courtesy of the Barnhill Collection, Pack Memorial Library, Asheville, North Carolina. Collection of Cary F. Poole.

A 42-ton Climax has brought an excursion train to a stop near the summit of Mount Mitchell. The tourists enjoy a short layover before the descent back down the mountain. Courtesy of the North Carolina Collection, Pack Memorial Library, Asheville, North Carolina.

the tourists boarded Train #21 for a short trip back to Asheville. While in Asheville, the excursioners completed their visit to the region with a comfortable stay at the Langren Hotel.

The Mount Mitchell Railroad employed a fleet of six Climax locomotives to alternately push and pull the excursion trains. The coaches used on the railroad appeared somewhat crude in appearance but were local in origin. They were constructed in the Southern Railway Asheville yard for the Mount Mitchell narrow gauge railroad.

Tourist trains continued from 1913 until 1918, when federal pressure forced curtailment of the excursion in favor of spruce lumber removal. The government was in the midst of a massive airplane development program for World War I, and spruce was used in the wing and fuselage construction.

In 1920 the Perley & Crockett Lumber Company ceased timber activity in the area; however, the Mount Mitchell Scenic Railroad was organized to resume excursions to the summit of Mount Mitchell. In 1921 the line ceased operations when it was determined that upkeep for a toll road was less costly than for the railroad. Upon completion of the toll road, the tracks were removed for their scrap value.

The toll road, though less expensive to operate than the railroad, was not without its own share of problems. Considering the toll road was constructed largely over a former narrow gauge railroad bed, the road was not very wide. In order to prevent accidents, traffic was limited to one direction each half day of operation. In the mornings the traffic was allowed to ascend the mountain to the summit. At noon, the traffic flow was reversed and only cars moving down the mountain were allowed to operate.

The location is Terrell's Depot (between Ridgecrest and Black Mountain, North Carolina) as a Climax locomotive proceeds to push an excursion train up to the summit of Mount Mitchell. Courtesy of the Presbyterian Historical Foundation.

A Climax locomotive is pushing a string of six coaches toward the summit of Mount Mitchell. The train has just traveled through one of nine switchbacks located on the line. Courtesy of the Barnhill Collection, Pack Memorial Library, Asheville, North Carolina.

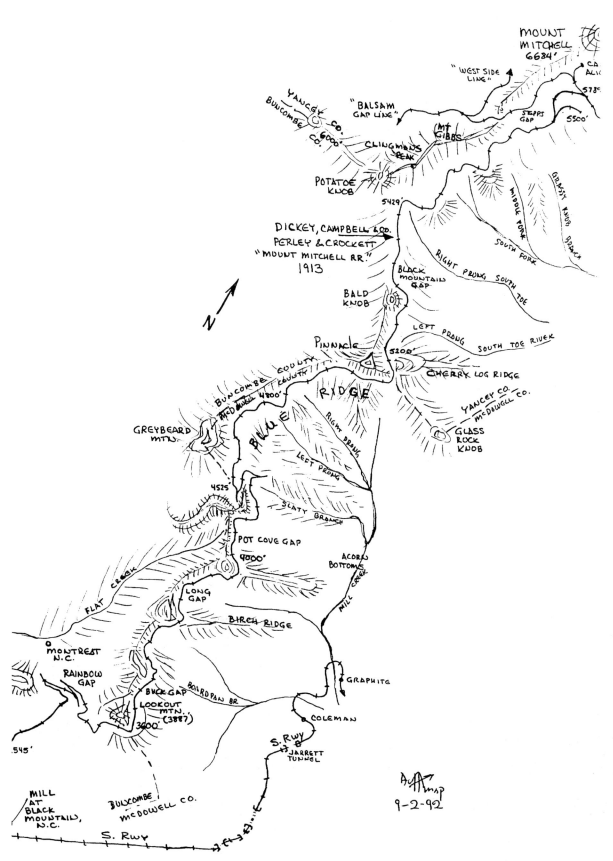

The Mount Mitchell Railroad line is illustrated as it makes its way north to near the summit of Mount Mitchell from its southern connection with the Southern Railway at Black Mountain, North Carolina. Courtesy of Tom Fetters.

TENNESSEE & NORTH CAROLINA RAILROADS

The corporate title "Tennessee & North Carolina Railroad" was an often used designation for four railroads which shared, at one time or another, the same name.

Of the four railroads, one did not serve North Carolina and will not be covered in this volume. The volume will chart the corporate histories of the other three railroads.

Two of the railroads to be included operated solely within North Carolina. Only one railroad out of the four was true to the state names contained in the title. That railroad operated from Newport, Tennessee, south to Crestmont, North Carolina. It will be the first of the three discussed within this chapter.

Newport, Tennessee, to Crestmont, North Carolina

Originally, the line was financed by J. B. Hart and J. J. Holloway of Clarksburg, West Virginia, both of whom had controlling interests in the North Carolina Timber & Land Company. Holloway became the first president, and Hart served as the corporate secretary.

The Tennessee & North Carolina Railroad was incorporated by Tennessee on March 6, 1900, and in North Carolina exactly three years later. A merger of the two charters took place on June 27, 1911.

The track work began soon after chartering on the Tennessee side by the company's own track crews. The Tennessee & North Carolina Railroad inter-changed with the Southern Railway on the southeast side of Newport. The line continued in a southerly direction for approximately 21 miles until it reached Crestmont. The tracks were completed to Crestmont by September 1902. The rail was laid in 55- to 60-pound rail.

Most of the crews employed to construct the line were locals who had settled these mountainous areas several generations prior to the arrival of the railroad and loggers. One interesting employment trend was the hiring of Native Americans from the Cherokee Nation to help in the construction. The line ran relatively close to the Eastern Band of the Cherokee reservation, and some members of that reservation were employed by the Tennessee & North Carolina Railroad as laborers and track workers.

A two-mile extension had been completed from Waterville to Crestmont by the Champion Lumber Company. The Tennessee & North Carolina Railroad held trackage rights on this section of track, and it represented the largest extent of trackage for the railroad.

Eventually Hart and Holloway sold their interests in the railroad to James Estate of Pennsylvania. Estate, in turn, sold the railroad to the Whitmer Company, which was owned and operated by William Whitmer and his sons.

The Whitmers controlled at various times the Pigeon River Lumber Company, Champion Fibre, and

2†	6k	4m	Mls.	Stations	1†	3k	5m
PM	AM	AM	——	Leave Arrive	AM	PM	PM
2:00	8:00	4:45	0	Newport Jct.	7:45	6:15	5:10
2:13	8:08	4:58	4	Edwina........	7:15	6:02	4:55
2:25	8:16	5:07	7	Wilton Sprgs	7:06	5:52	4:47
2:31	8:21	5:12	9	Denton........	7:00	5:48	4:41
2:46	8:34	5:25	13	Bluffton......	6:46	5:38	4:31
2:51	8:40	5:30	15	Hartford......	6:38	5:30	4:25
2:58	8:45	5:35	16	Naillon........	6:25	5:20	4:20
3:10	8:50	5:40	18	Browns,Tenn	6:20	5:15	4:15
3:20	8:56	5:45	19	Waterville,NC	6:15	5:10	4:10
3:40	9:10	5:55	21	Crestmont...	6:00	5:00	4:00
PM	AM	AM	——	Arrive Leave	AM	PM	PM

The 1910 timetable lists six trains a day running between Newport Junction, Tennessee, and Crestmont, North Carolina. Courtesy of *The Official Railway Guide.*

The #100 was a Baldwin-built 4-4-0 American photographed in Newport, Tennessee, in August 1932. Collection of Harold K. Vollrath.

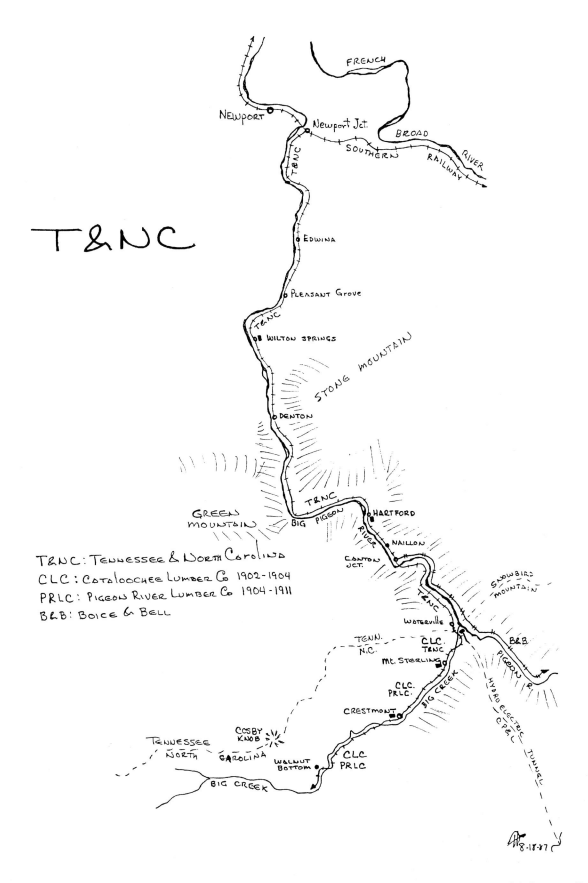

The Tennessee & North Carolina Railroad, the only one of four with that name which actually operated in both states, closely followed the Pigeon River for the majority of its route. Courtesy of Tom Fetters.

geon River Lumber Company, Champion Fibre, and the Champion Lumber Company.

For the casual observer, it was not an easy task to determine whether equipment belonged to the Tennessee & North Carolina Railroad, the Pigeon River Railroad, or the Champion Lumber Company, since all—at one time or another—were controlled by the Whitmer Company. It was generally believed at the height of the traffic that the Tennessee & North Carolina Railroad had five locomotives, three coaches, two mail/baggage cars, and various other forms of rolling stock. Surprisingly, the railroad also leased 20 stock cars from the Mather Stock Car Company.

The railroad was developed to serve the economic needs of Cocke County, Tennessee, and Haywood County, North Carolina. Most of the economic development centered on timber removal and the sawing of lumber. Even though the Tennessee & North Carolina Railroad was adequately serving its intended purpose, the railroad could not escape receivership. By court order, the railroad was sold on June 7, 1920, to pay creditors. It was at this time the railroad emerged from receivership.

The two new owners, C. Boice and J. W. Bell, also operated the Boice Hardwood Company, which was located at Hartford, Tennessee. This mill was already located along the route of the railroad, so the new owners had a third rail installed from Canton Junction to Hartford to permit their narrow gauge trains to run directly to the mill without having to transfer

A Boice Hardwood Company Shay locomotive is photographed at Hartfort, Tennessee. Photograph by G.P. Vance. Collection of C.K. Marsh, Jr.

their logs to standard gauge cars.

In 1926 the Tennessee & North Carolina Railroad expanded its railroad interests when it bid on and was accepted to operate the Smoky Mountain Railroad.

Most railroads experienced wrecks or mishaps which were truly horrible incidents. These incidents often became embedded in the public's mind in the form of songs, poems, or local folklore. While the Tennessee & North Carolina Railroad had its share of mishaps and wrecks, one incident had a comical ending and is worth retelling.

The story begins on a cold, wintry morning at four o'clock. The fireman and engineer had stoked the fire and oiled around their 2-6-2 Prairie locomotive. Since it was a cold morning, they went to the Junction depot to warm up. Soon the conductor and the railroad superintendent stopped by the depot to check on the train orders for the day. The superintendent inquired into the location of the locomotive, since it was not parked outside the depot. The fireman and engineer were shocked to find the train missing as they ran outside to verify the superintendent's statement. The four men quickly rounded up the only available piece of transportation—a handcar—and left Newport in hot pursuit.

At Edwina, a shop owner had just opened his doors for business when the four out-of-breath railroad employees rolled by. He was able to inform them that the train had steamed by at five o'clock in the morning and that the crew members were being careless in the performance of

The Tennessee & North Carolina Railroad had 21 miles of track between Newport, Tennessee, and Crestmont, North Carolina. Courtesy of *The Official Railway Guide.*

their jobs. They had not blown for the road crossings in the area.

The four railroad employees again were in pursuit of the crewless train. As they approached Wilton Hill, the train was near a halt, a full seven miles from where it had started its journey.

In Haywood County, North Carolina, the railroad operated trackage through 23,000 acres of timber owned by the Boice Hardwood Company. The trackage out of Crestmont, North Carolina, employed both switchbacks and inclined tracks to facilitate the removal of the timber.

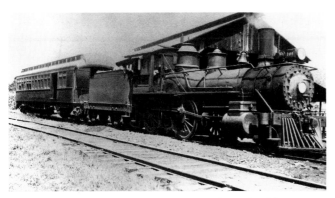

The T&NC #100 was photographed in Newport, Tennessee, in August 1932. Collection of Harold K. Vollrath.

The band mill at Hartford operated until 1931, at which time it had cut 130 million board feet of timber.

By the early 1930s, the forests had largely been depleted and the Tennessee & North Carolina Railroad was having to perform more and more on the basis of a common carrier rather than a logging railroad. As revenues dropped, particularly after the closing of the mill in 1931, steam passenger service curtailed in favor of a gas-powered bus.

By 1931 deficits had reached $17,000. On July 12, 1937, an application for abandonment was filed with the ICC. Due to local protests, the railroad proposed to continue operations until January 1, 1938. This allowed local timber and lumber interests a chance to ship any remaining products out before abandonment.

Andrews to Hayesville, North Carolina

The smallest of the three T&NC Railroads to be covered in this publication is a line which ran from Andrews to Hayesville, North Carolina. The railroad was incorporated in March 1919 and carried the title Carolina & Georgia Railroad. That corporate title was used untill 1922, when the railroad changed its name to the Tennessee & North Carolina Railroad.

The #80 is under steam moving log racks in Hayesville, North Carolina, during October 1947. Collection of Harold K. Vollrath.

The Tennessee & North Carolina #105, a 2-6-2 Baldwin-built Prairie, was photographed at Andrews, North Carolina, on July 13, 1936. Photograph by William Monypeny. Collection of Frank Ardrey.

The #105 was photographed again in Andrews in December 1946. Collection of Harold K. Vollrath.

This Tennessee & North Carolina 2-6-0 Mogul was photographed in Hayesville, North Carolina, in 1938. Collection of Norman Williams.

Tennessee & North Carolina #8, a 2-6-2 Prairie, was photographed in Andrews, North Carolina, in 1948. Collection of Tom King.

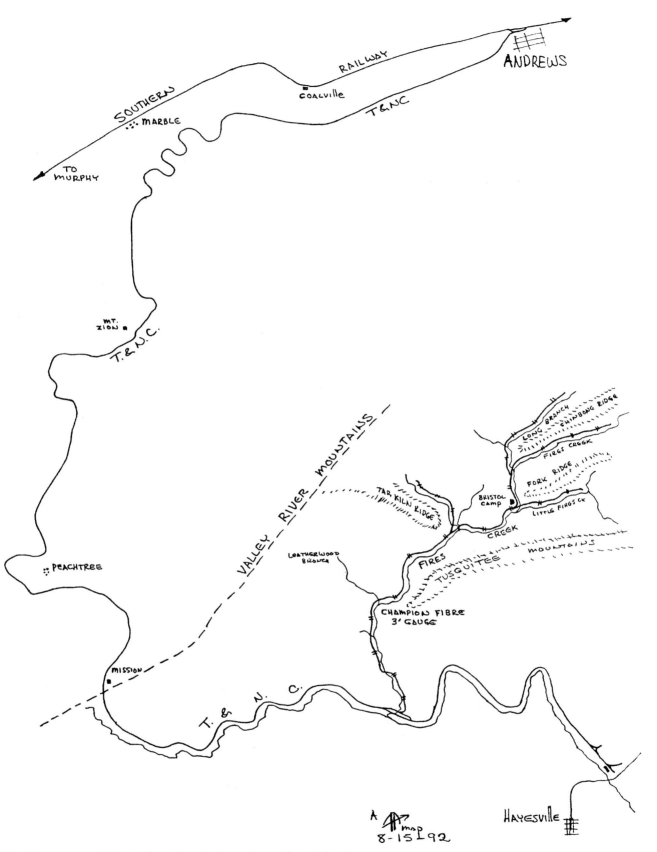

The Tennessee & North Carolina Railroad paralleled the Southern Railway line for a short distance out of Andrews, then turned southward to avoid the Valley River Mountains on its way to Hayesville, North Carolina. Courtesy of Tom Fetters.

The railroad was standard gauge and operated approximately 20 miles of track. While the railroad was a common carrier, the principal commodity was timber to be taken to Andrews, where it would be sawed into lumber.

The line ran southwesterly from Andrews and followed the Valley River until it reached the community of Marble. From Andrews to Marble the line paralleled the Southern Railway's Murphy Branch on the opposite bank of the Valley River. At Marble the line veered southward until it reached the community of Peachtree. Here the line swung sharply to the east in order to clear a mountain range and then continued in an easterly pattern until it reached Hayesville.

The railroad borrowed the #1925, a two-truck Shay, from the Graham County Railroad for a period of approximately six months. During the short stay on the line, the locomotive was wrecked and later had to be overhauled before it could return to use on the Graham County Railroad.

The T&NC connected with a Champion Fibre Company logging line just north of Hayesville. The Champion line was a 3' narrow gauge and ran in a northeasterly direction from the connection. A small community by the name of Fires Creek, occupied primarily by Champion Fibre employees, was located on the narrow gauge line. This particular line was temporary storage for steam equipment from another Champion Fibre operation which interchanged with the Graham County Railroad. When the Champion Fibre line closed down in Graham County, the equipment was stored until it could be disposed of as scrap. However, World War II arrived and the equipment was not only spared, but returned to service on other 3' lines. This unusual circumstance prevented a 3' Climax from being scrapped. Today, it resides at the Cradle of Forestry Museum near Brevard, North Carolina.

The line was abandoned in approximately 1959, leaving the community of Hayesville without rail service.

West Canton to Sunburst, North Carolina

In 1907 Peter Thompson founded the Champion

A Climax locomotive at Pigeon Run in 1914 in Haywood County, North Carolina. Courtesy of the Austin-Brooks Collection, Ramsey Library, UNC-Asheville.

Fibre Company when he purchased 1,000 acres of land on the Pigeon River. Thompson purchased the property for $5.00 per acre and immediately established plans to build a mill on the acquired land. The newly formed company was constructed at a location referred to by the locals as Pigeon Ford, known today as Canton, North Carolina.

The original intent was to construct a water flume to haul logs to the mill at Pigeon Ford. The slope of the surrounding area was too gentle to force the timber down the flume, and the plan was soon abandoned.

The Champion Fibre Company next considered constructing their own railroad to move the pulpwood to the mill. After much research and cost evaluation, the construction was ruled out as being too costly to fund. Champion Fibre then negotiated with the Whitmer Company of Philadelphia, Pennsylvania, to construct a railroad and keep the Pigeon Ford mill supplied with pulpwood. The Whitmer Company was known locally as the Champion Lumber Company and did indeed supply the Champion mill with pulpwood for many years.

A contractor from Knoxville, Tennessee, was employed to construct the railroad. Mr. Oliver was known for his construction skills and had developed a national reputation from his work on the Panama Canal. The work was sublet from Oliver to the Yandell brothers, also of Knoxville, Tennessee. The proposed length was to be 20 miles of track running south from Canton to Sunburst.

After overextending itself financially, the Whitmer Company entered into court-ordered receivership and the newly reorganized company became the Suncrest Lumber Company. Supposedly the "Sun" part of the name originated from Sunburst and the "Crest" part from Crestmont, site of other Champion timbering activity. From this time on, the railroad was financially tied to the Champion Fibre Company of Canton, North Carolina, and became known as the Pigeon River Railroad.

A large mill with a double-band saw was projected for construction at Sunburst, with spruce to be the principal timber targeted for cutting. Pulpwood would also be processed for shipment to the sulphite mill at Canton.

When the original charter was issued by the state of North Carolina, the two termini listed in the document were Canton and Sunburst. Sunburst was to be located south of Canton approximately 16 miles. In the charter, Sunburst was recognized as a location at the three forks of the west prong of the Pigeon River.

The Whitmer Company encountered an interesting problem when local land owners refused to sell on the initial price quoted. The local owners felt the presence of a common carrier railroad would escalate prices, and they were determined not to sell the

The community of Sunburst, North Carolina. The entire location is now under water due to the construction of a dam to fill Lake Logan. Courtesy of Canton Area Museum.

property until the price met with their satisfaction. To escape the impending necessity to ship logs via common carrier on the Pigeon River Railroad, a good deal of corporate maneuvering resulted in the moving of the town of Sunburst four miles up the line closer to Canton. The terminus points remained intact according to the state charter, but the railroad had shortened its common carrier track by four miles. The four miles of track in question were then listed as a private railroad, and rates were set at what the market could bear.

The former site on the three forks was renamed Spruce, and this ended the problem of having to quote common carrier rates. The unwilling sellers referred to the new Sunburst as the "Bastard Sunburst." The old Sunburst, now named Spruce, was referred to as the "Legitimate Sunburst."

The new Sunburst soon became a model sawmill town with a population of over 500 residents. Of the 500 residents, approximately 100 were blacks, who worked either for the railroad or in the sawmill. The town was of such a size that a "colored" school was organized for the children of the black community.

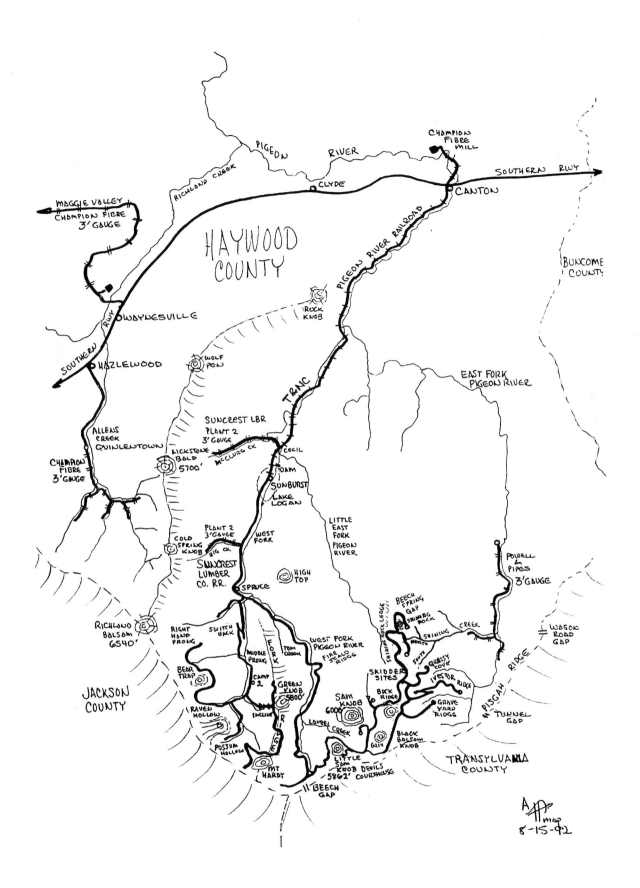

Connected with the Southern Railway in Canton, North Carolina, the Tennessee & North Carolina Railroad spread southward through Haywood County. Courtesy of Tom Fetters.

A Champion Lumber Company Shay, #7 is photographed near Spruce, North Carolina. The photograph was taken by G.P. Vance. Collection of Doug Walker.

A Pigeon River Railroad (Tennessee & North Carolina) Shay and Climax are photographed at Sunburst, North Carolina. Courtesy of Jim King.

Enrollment at the black school consisted of about 20 students, with the first through the seventh grades being taught. School books had to be purchased by the students, and library books were checked out from the white school.

An interesting point regarding Sunburst was the number of telephones in the community. For a village of 500 residents, over 100 telephones existed in the area. The system was so extensive it required the services of a full-time telephone operator to handle the volume of calls. Telephones were also installed along the tracks so the crews could mark their progress with the railroad office and call attention to problems trackside.

In 1913, *Southern Lumberman* reported on the production levels for the sawmills at Sunburst. It was reported 135,000 to 175,000 board feet of lumber were turned out daily, with a projected five million board feet a month as a quota. It was also projected 60,000 carloads of lumber would pass out of all the mountains of Western North Carolina per year.

During the height of World War I, spruce was needed for the production of airplanes, and the U.S. government went to any length to insure a steady supply. In 1918, 181 men from an Army engineering company out of Camp Wheeler, near Macon, Georgia, arrived to help facilitate the increased spruce production. The engineers constructed several additional miles of logging tracks to help reach previously inaccessible stands of spruce. This construction on a private railroad was approved by the U.S. War Department as being necessary for the increased production of aircraft.

A typical schedule was for the trains to leave Sunburst at 7:15 a.m. and arrive in West Canton at 8:30 a.m. On the return trip, the train left West Canton at 10:35 a.m. and arrived back at Sunburst at 11:50 a.m. The schedule operated every day except Sunday.

As with other Pigeon River Railroad operations, equipment was often shuffled between the various lines. It was not uncommon to observe rolling stock on the Canton to Sunburst line one month and then see the same piece of equipment operating out of Newport, Tennessee, the very next month. Shay-geared locomotives proved to be the most popular type of engine and were employed not only on the passenger runs but for the logging operations as well.

In addition to the Shays, the T&NC Railroad owned a jitney, which was used in limited passenger service. This jitney was a flanged Ford-built bus which could handle 10 to 12 passengers.

As with most logging operations, wrecks and mishaps were commonplace. One accident involved two Shays that were working a string of loaded log cars, one locomotive on the head-end pulling the train, and the second engine on the rear, pushing. The crews adjusted the throttles of the two engines through the use of whistle signals. As the lead engine applied more and more throttle, the pushing engine in the rear slipped between the rails. The lead engine proceeded to pull the loaded cars and the derailed engine up the mountain for a short distance. It took a few minutes before the lead crew heard and understood the distress call from the trailing crew to stop the engine.

With the railroad operating two divisions, both along the Pigeon River, thought soon turned to the idea of connecting the two lines. The idea would involve constructing a line north from Canton along the route of the Pigeon River until it could connect with the other Pigeon River Railroad at or near the Tennessee state line. A suitable pass was not found, and the idea never materialized.

The Tennessee & North Carolina Railroad lasted from 1906 until 1933, when the last rails were removed. Today, the site of Sunburst is under water due to the construction of the dam on Lake Logan. Most visitors find it difficult to imagine that the former site of a town of 500 residents has simply vanished under the lake.

GRAHAM COUNTY RAILROAD
BUFFALO & SNOWBIRD RAILROAD
CHAMPION FIBRE CO. RAILROAD

The Graham County Railroad was located in its namesake county in Western North Carolina. The line had one connection to the outside world, at Topton, North Carolina, with the Southern Railway on the Murphy Branch.

The first railroad in the general area of Graham County was the Snowbird Valley Railroad. The original purpose for the line was to tap the timber reserves located on the Buffalo and Snowbird mountains, which formed the boundary between North Carolina and Tennessee. It was constructed by the Kanawha Hardwood Company, which first employed splash dams and then attempted to use a steam-powered tractor to remove the timber. When both the splash dams and steam tractor proved impractical, the decision was made to construct a railroad for timber removal. The line was constructed in a 3' gauge along the Snowbird Creek. The line failed, however, in 1917, and the track was removed and sold to the Republic of France. There, the rails were used in the war effort against Kaiser Wilhelm.

On February 27, 1905, a charter was issued to the Graham County Railroad Company for a line to connect the county seat of Robbinsville to the Southern Railway at Topton. It took five years before any construction started, and a capital stock issue of $150,000 was authorized to fund the railroad.

In 1910 the Whiting Company of Philadelphia, Pennsylvania, bought the entire town of Robbinsville as reported in the *Southern Lumberman*. With the sale of the town, an electric plant was planned and the Whiting company projected the employment of 1,500 men in the logging and lumber business. It was another six years before the construction commenced on the railroad.

In 1916 the effort was intensified and construction began. The Whiting Company proceeded with the construction from Robbinsville to Topton. Later in the year, the construction came to a quick halt when a strange quirk of nature put the railroad out of business. The Whiting Company had purchased a used Baldwin-built 2-6-2 rod locomotive for use on the line. The locomotive was in need of repairs and was sent to

Asheville, North Carolina, in order to be overhauled by the Southern Railway shop mechanics. It was in July 1916 that the horrible flood struck and wiped out three of the four railroads into Asheville. It was also in this flood that the Graham County Railroad engine was washed downstream, never to be found. With the loss of its sole piece of motive power, the railroad was forced to halt construction on the line.

The early 1920s brought both the Bemis Lumber Company of Fishing Hawk, West Virginia, and the Champion Fibre Company of Canton, North Carolina, to the area. Both companies arranged for a mutual agreement for the exploitation of the timber

MAP OF THE
GRAHAM COUNTY RAILROAD

LEGEND
——— Graham County Railroad

The Graham County Railroad is shown in perspective with the Southern Railway's Murphy Branch. Courtesy of Pack Memorial Library, Asheville, North Carolina.

Graham County Railroad #1925 is photographed in Robbinsville, North Carolina, in October 1959. The locomotive is a Lima-built three-truck Shay. Collection of Harold K. Vollrath.

reserves. Bemis owned the title to the land and hard-woods along the Buffalo, Santeellah, and Snowbird creeks. Champion received the rights to the softwoods and hemlocks, which it intended to use in the paper-making process at its Canton, North Carolina, plant.

The unique arrangement also allowed both companies to develop their own railroads in the local vicinity. The Bemis Company had utilized a standard gauge line in West Virginia and proposed to continue to use its equipment from that location. Champion, on the other hand, operated several 3' gauge lines in Western North Carolina and preferred to continue to use narrow gauge equipment.

The Graham County Railroad was finally completed in 1925, with the tracks running from Robbinsville to Topton, North Carolina. That year also marked the delivery of a new 70-ton two-truck Shay from the Lima Locomotive Works. The locomotive was numbered for the year of its manufacture, #1925, and served the Graham County Railroad throughout the line's existence.

Bemis's new operation was labeled the Buffalo & Snowbird Railroad, yet no equipment was ever lettered in such a fashion. In this manner, freight charges were billed separately from the Graham County Railroad, which was listed as a common carrier.

Bemis was busy expanding its operation by re-laying the track over the old Snowbird Valley Railroad right-of-way. In addition to the Snowbird Valley segment, track was also laid in the Dick Branch section of the county.

While Bemis was busy expanding its operation, Champion Fibre was just as busy increasing its own track mileage. Champion extended its line into a new joint operation labeled "Junction." This junction was a dual-gauged interchange which facilitated loading and unloading between the narrow and standard gauge railroads.

The peak of activity on the line was in the late 1920s and early 1930s. It was at this peak period of business that the Graham County Railroad served as the only avenue of transportation for the county. Sawed lumber and pulpwood moved south from the Bemis mill at Robbinsville to Topton for shipment out on the Southern Railway. Boxcars of vegetables, general merchandise, hardware, and household items headed north to the residents of Robbinsville.

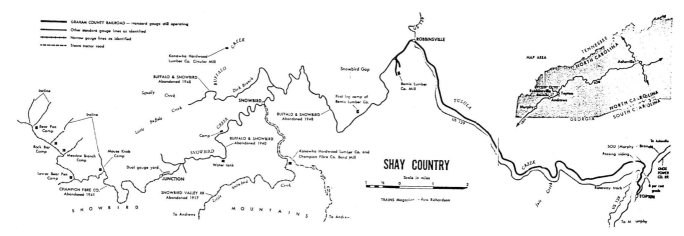

The map above illustrates the Graham County Railroad, a standard gauge operation which connected Topton and Robbinsville, North Carolina, and the narrow gauge feeder lines which stretched westward from Robbinsville. Courtesy of *Trains* magazine.

The Champion Fibre line from Junction running west to Meadow Camp Branch and Bear Pen Camp was abandoned in 1941. During World War II, Champion Fibre moved its equipment to Fires Creek, North Carolina, on the company-owned Tennessee & North Carolina Railroad. After the T&NC was abandoned in 1959, the Climax and a Shay went to work on the Ely-Thomas logging line in West Virginia. Today the Climax is preserved at the Cradle of Forestry Museum near Brevard, North Carolina. Mars Hill College History Professor Dr. Harley Jolley and a student were instrumental in tracking down the locomotive and subsequently having it returned and preserved in Western North Carolina. The locomotive, along with a couple of log cars and an American log loader, serves as a interpretive display.

Typical operations involved the trains running backwards from Robbinsville to Topton. This practice was due to the lack of a wye on the line. The conductor rode in the caboose in order to observe grade crossings for the engineer, who was at the end of the

The #1926 works the Bemis Lumber Company yard in January 1963. Collection of Tom L. Sink.

Narrow gauge lines ran west from Robbinsville, North Carolina, and were used to haul timber for the Bemis Lumber Company. This narrow gauge Climax was originally constructed in 1915 for Champion Fibre Company and eventually ended up in West Virginia on the Ely-Thomas Lumber Company line. Today the engine is preserved at the Cradle of Forestry Museum near Pisgah Forest, North Carolina. Collection of C.K. Marsh, Jr.

train in the locomotive. If water was needed for the Shay, more often than not, a nearby creek was used to replenish the tender. A typical work week consisted of taking freight to Topton three days a week and working the Bemis plant or repairing the equipment on the remaining days.

The Graham County Railroad standard gauge operation had a fondness for Shay locomotives. For many years, the railroad was a haven for railfans who wanted to study, photograph, and simply observe the mechanism of the Shays. The Graham County Railroad was also one of the few lines in which the disposition of most of its motive power could be traced. The #1925 was purchased new. The #1926 was obtained from the Tallassee Power Company. The number "3229" appeared on the side of the original #1926 after a runaway log car damaged the smokebox and front-end of the #1926. Spare parts from a narrow gauge Shay, #3229, were used to patch up the #1926.

The line held on until the mid-1960s, when the day-to-day existence of the railroad was precarious at best. The timber had been largely removed, and freight hauling was the only business keeping the line open.

In 1966 a new lease on life appeared for the railroad. An agreement had been reached between three parties: Bemis Lumber Co., the Graham County Railroad, and Government Services, Inc., a concession vendor. Together, the three groups proposed an excursion railroad to utilize the interest in Shays and

The Graham County Railroad and the Southern Railroad exchange freight at Graham County Junction on the Murphy Branch. Collection of Ronald Deitz.

The Graham County #1926 was built by Lima in the same year as its number. The locomotive is a three-truck superheated Shay. The photograph was taken in December 1961. Collection of Harold K. Vollrath.

Hassinger Lumber Company #4 is shown while still under that company's service. The #4 went to the Graham County Railroad in 1929, and was declared inoperable in 1940 when a night watchman let the engine run dry. The locomotive was cut up for scrap in 1947. During scrapping, the cylinders proved to be so heavy as to turn over a log loader being used to lift them. The #4 was a four-truck, 120-ton Shay locomotive built in 1913, c/n 2700. Collection of Doug Walker.

With the rear cars partially obscured by the exhaust and the low cloud ceiling, the #1926 is photographed in January 1961. Photograph by Tom L. Sink.

The Graham County #1926 is shown with a short string of cars in August 1962. Photograph by Tom L. Sink.

The #1926 is "spotting" cars in the small yard at Topton, North Carolina. Photograph by John Krause.

Looking down the Nantahala Gorge in August 1972, a Graham County Railroad locomotive pulls a single tank car to Robbinsville, North Carolina. Photograph by Tom L. Sink.

steam-powered locomotives. The new operation was called the Bear Creek Junction Railroad and quickly picked up a loyal following of steam aficionados.

Luck, however, was to be cruel and dealt the Graham County Railroad a bad hand. In 1968 a wreck occurred in which there were no fatalities, but some injuries. The last run was made in 1970 and was filmed by a CBS camera crew.

In 1973 a second group of investors attempted to resurrect the Graham County Railroad with a tourist division called the Bear Creek Junction. The tourist operation took riders from a new depot near the Bear Creek Baptist Church to the interchange with the Southern Railway near Topton and back again to the new depot. The #1925 was spruced up and sported the name "Ed Collins" under the cab window. Ed Collins was a lifelong employee of the railroad who had started his career in 1928, only three years after the line was opened. He was a warm friend to the many railfans who visited the line over the years and was noted for his hymn singing and scripture quoting while at the throttle.

On March 28, 1978, disaster struck again when floods destroyed portions of the line and removed two bridges between Bear Creek Junction and Robbinsville. With the bridges out, the Graham County

Railroad was prevented from being a freight hauler, since it could no longer switch the Bemis mill. June 29, 1978, marked the last run for the #1925 on the Graham County Railroad.

Local interests tried one last time to reorganize the railroad but were unsuccessful. Due to conflicting political views and a lack of concensus on what direction the new project was to take, the railroad failed for the last time.

In 1987 the rails were pulled from Topton to Robbinsville. All that remain are the station at Bear Creek Junction and the stone masonry retaining wall, which marked the small three-track interchange with the Southern Railway. The #1925 is currently being restored at the North Carolina Transportation Museum in Spencer, North Carolina.

The Graham County Railroad had two diesel locomotives in its corporate history. The GE 70-tonner shown above is an ex-Savannah State Docks locomotive. The photograph was taken in October 1974 by Tom L. Sink.

Graham County Railroad #17, a SW-8, is photographed at Bear Creek Junction, midpoint between Topton and Robbinsville, North Carolina. Photograph by Kent S. Roberts.

APPALACHIAN RAILWAY

The Appalachian Railway was a standard gauge short line which interchanged with the Southern Railway at Ela, North Carolina, on the famed Murphy Branch. In many ways, the railway was one of the more unusual of the logging lines due to the line's having been constructed through tribal lands of the Cherokee Nation.

J. C. Arbogast and B. M. Yeager went before the Tribal Council of the Eastern Band of the Cherokee Nation in 1906 to ask for a right-of-way through reservation lands. A major concern of the council was that the railroad would open up the reservation to possible encroachment by outside forces and influences. After much discussion on the part of the council, permission was granted for the proposed railroad.

A portion of the line ran from Ela to Ravenford, North Carolina, through the boundaries of the reservation. The portion of the line through the reservation was approximately ten miles in length; and an additional ten miles, which branched out from Smokemont, North Carolina, was obtained from private owners. The line which extended north of Ravenford was constructed on private property purchased from the land owners.

Construction started in 1906, and the line was built steadily until it reached the Cherokee in 1908. When the line reached that point, the original owners had exhausted their finances and construction ceased.

The Parson Pulp & Lumber Company, located at Ravenford, created a subsidiary operation, the Appalachian Railway Company, to resume construction and to take over daily operations. The line remained under the control of the Parson Pulp & Lumber Company until the railroad's demise.

By 1912 the line was extended to Ravenford. It is interesting to note that final action was approved jointly by the Cherokee Tribal Council and the Department of the Interior. Those signing the petition were simply acknowledging the construction of an already largely functioning railroad. The signers of the petition were James Welch, Chief of the Eastern Band of the Cherokee Nation; James Kyrelka, Superintendent of the reservation, and James Pierce, Commissioner of Indian Affairs. Two additional witnesses

of the signing were James Oocuma, Chairman of the Council, and James Tabquitte, Clerk of the Council.

The petition provided for a 50-foot right-of-way for the railroad and for reimbursement for any property disturbed by construction. The petition further called upon the railroad to be a common carrier and to haul passengers for as long as the line operated. This provision is what caused considerable consternation on the part of the reservation's inhabitants. A portion of the members of the reservation preferred to live an isolationist lifestyle, while others preferred contact with the outside world. The group wishing to make contacts outside the reservation finally won out, however, and the petition was signed.

Another provision contained in the petition was a specific route for the railroad from Ela to Ravenford. The projected route would be alongside the Ocono Lufty (White River). Lastly, the reservation members insisted upon return of the land once the railroad ceased operations.

Shortly after 1912, the Champion Fibre Company pushed a narrow gauge line farther north to Smokemont, North Carolina. This increased logging traffic significantly on the Appalachian Railway since Parson, with a mill at Ravenford, and Champion Fibre, with a mill at Smokemont, both contributed to outbound traffic on the line.

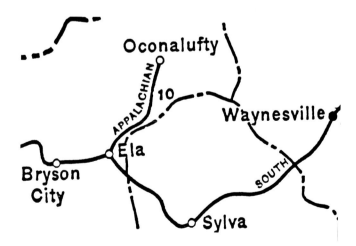

The Appalachian Railroad ran ten miles north of its connection at Ela with the Southern Railway to Oconalufty, well into the Reservation of the Eastern Band of the Cherokee Nation. Collection of Pack Memorial Library, Asheville, North Carolina.

The operations of the Appalachian Railway came to an abrupt halt when the federal government proceeded with the acquisition of land to establish the Great Smoky Mountains National Park. The federal government used its right of eminent domain to proceed with the purchasing of the required lands. This, in effect, brought an end to logging operations, and the holding company received $50,000 in compensation for the railroad. By 1935 the rails had been removed, and the railroad bed became State Highway 107, which still serves the same communities as did the railroad. The roadbed through the reservation of the Eastern Band of the Cherokee Nation reverted back to the people of that reservation as stipulated in the original charter.

The above photograph was taken in Canton, North Carolina, in 1938 after the Appalachian Railroad had ceased operations. At this time, the engine had been sold to Champion Fibre, and it served that company until 1945. In that year, a watchman allowed the engine to freeze and it was cut up in Canton. Photograph by Norman Williams.

TUCKASEGEE AND SOUTHEASTERN RAILROAD

This three-truck Climax was photographed in Sylva, North Carolina. The Tuckasegee & Southeastern Railroad used narrow gauge equipment on the feeder lines which ran south of East La Porte, North Carolina. The feeder lines brought in cut timber from the surrounding mountains. It was sawed into lumber in East La Porte and transported by standard gauge boxcars to Sylva. Collection of Tom L. Sink.

The above flange-equipped automobile was used by the Blackwood Lumber Company doctor to visit his patients. The rails were the only form of transportation into some of the isolated communities. Courtesy of Western Carolina University.

The #1 is shown in a flooded creek near Sylva, North Carolina, on August 30, 1941. Photograph by Herbert Gibson. Collection of Tom King.

The crew of Shay #1 poses next to the East La Porte garage. Today, the site of East La Porte is a grassy field. Courtesy of Western Carolina University.

The Tuckasegee & Southeastern Railroad was a standard gauge operation which ran from Sylva south to the community of East La Porte, North Carolina. The railroad controlled a franchise which would have allowed it to extend a full 35 miles to Lake Toxaway. This extension was never constructed. The total distance of the line which was constructed was 12.5 miles.

Narrow gauge feeder lines helped transport the timber to the mill at East La Porte. At East La Porte the logs were transferred from the narrow gauge rolling stock to standard gauge stock for the journey north to Sylva.

The fortune of the T&SE Railroad always depended on the business fortunes of the Blackwood Lumber Company. During the height of operations in the late 1920s, East La Porte had a double-band mill operation with 100 workers.

Passenger service was inaugurated in 1922 with a Packard school bus equipped with flange wheels. Local residents remembered the jitney had a capacity of 12 to 14 passengers.

Since the small community of Cullowhee was fairly isolated, the T&SE Railroad served as a major artery for transportation for the Western Carolina Normal College. As part of a probable public relations ploy, the local college students were allowed to ride the freights free of charge. It should be noted, however, that female students were prohibited from partaking of this form of transportation. Local residents often observed college faculty members riding the freights headed north to Sylva. In many cases the faculty members had to ride on top of the boxcars due to the full capacity from the loaded lumber. It was

reported the accommodations were better on the trip south since the cars were generally shipped empty to the mill at East La Porte.

During the 1932-33 academic year, the state legislature was forced to slash faculty and staff salaries at Western Carolina Normal College. During this period, the college president was often observed riding the roof of a lumber-laden boxcar. One trip to meet

The Tuckasegee & Southeastern #1 is under steam at Sylva, North Carolina, in September 1941. The Shay was built by Lima in 1922, c/n 3172. Collection of Harold K. Vollrath.

with state legislators began in this fashion on the stretch from Cullowhee to Sylva. From Sylva he made the connection with the Southern and eventually arrived at his destination in Raleigh. It was later reported that the president of the college was successful in his mission to restore adequate funding for the institution.

With the closing of the Blackwood Lumber Company in 1946, the Tuckasegee & Southeastern Railroad ceased operations. As with most railroad abandonments, the rails were soon removed for their salvage value. Today, the former site of the community of East La Porte is an open field with few signs of its past. The locality is still referred to by the East La Porte name, but it is found on few state maps.

THE BEE TREE LUMBER COMPANY AND RAILROAD

One of the early locomotives on the Bee Tree Railroad was #118, a 4-4-0 American wood burner. Courtesy of the Presbyterian Historical Foundation.

An American 4-4-0, #18 is pushing an ACL flatcar near Swannanoa, North Carolina, circa 1910. Courtesy of the Presbyterian Historical Foundation.

Interior of the Craggy Lumber Company mill, owner of the Bee Tree Railroad. The mill was completely destroyed in the flood of 1916. Collection of Cary F. Poole.

A Shay and a Climax geared locomotive head a line of other equipment on the Bee Tree Railroad. Collection of Cary F. Poole.

Log cars used by the Bee Tree Railroad are shown in Swannanoa, North Carolina, in 1910. Courtesy of the Presbyterian Historical Foundation.

The crew of Shay #3 poses for their photograph in 1912. The crew members are, from left to right, Voll Pruitt, Will Dockett, and Charlie Buchanan. Mr. Pruitt was later recruited by the Southern Railway but remained loyal to the Craggy Lumber Company and moved with the company to Virginia. Collection of Cary F. Poole.

The Bee Tree Railroad was a logging line based near the small community of Copper's Station, later renamed Swannanoa.

In 1903 the small Craggy Lumber Company was founded. It later evolved into the Bee Tree Lumber Company. The right-of-way for the railroad was laid in 1910 to help in the removal of the timber. On November 8, 1910, the Craggy Lumber Company was declared bankrupt in a Charlotte, North Carolina, court.

The company assets were purchased in July 1911 by a group of Pennsylvania investors, and the sale included 10,000 acres for a total sale price of $160,000. In 1912 a larger mill was designed to replace the smaller mill and to handle the increased timbering. It was at this time the logging railroad operations commenced at full speed.

The line ran north from the Swannanoa Valley to the foot of the mountains which form the valley's northern rim. The line's connection with the Southern Railway was at the small community of Olivet, east of Asheville.

The new company also proposed building a large hotel and resort on the summit of Craggy Mountain. The purpose of the resort was to tap into the lucrative tourist market, which was booming at the time.

Logging operations continued from 1912 until 1916, when the devastating flood which so seriously affected Western North Carolina also spelled the doom of the Bee Tree Lumber Company. During the four years of timbering, large sections of timber had been removed. When the flood destroyed the mill, the company opted not to rebuild, but rather moved the entire operation to Nelson County, Virginia, and continued operations there for several more years.

Miss Catherine Pruett, whose father was an engineer on the Bee Tree, remembered her father was tempted by a job offer on the Southern Railway. However, he remained loyal to the Bee Tree Lumber Company and moved with the company to Virginia.

Today, the original roadbed exists as the foundation of an asphalted county road which leads to the base of the mountains where the logging railroad operations took place. The mountainous areas where the timber was removed between 1912 and 1916 now serve as a watershed area for Buncombe County.

LAUREL RIVER & HOT SPRINGS RAILROAD
MADISON COUNTY RAILROAD

In 1892 the owners of the New England Southern Timber & Land Company decided the best way to remove timber from large tracts of land in Madison County, North Carolina, was to utilize a railroad.

In May of 1892, the company held a meeting and the decision was made to construct the line up the Big Laurel and Foster creeks, since most of the accessible timber was located along those two bodies of water. The same meeting also produced the decision to build the line in a 2' gauge.

The initial line was to be constructed opposite the river from Hot Springs, North Carolina, to Tan Yard, through Gahagan Gap, to Little Hurricane Creek, to the Laurel River, up the Laurel River to Foster's Creek, and finally to Laurelton.

The capital raised was $150,000 divided into 3,000 shares. The first president elected was James Wyman of Lynn. Forty percent of the stock was owned locally, with the controlling interest belonging to the New England Southern Timber & Land Company.

The first year of construction was hampered by extremely severe weather. In light of the weather, crews were scaled back and work resumed only when the hard winter permitted.

With the completion of the wooden trestles, as well as an iron span, the railroad opened for business with 2.5 miles of track. The rail was 35 pound. An additional six miles of grading had been completed but never saw ties or rail laid.

While only 2.5 miles were laid in 1892-1893, the original charter called for ten miles of track. With the short distance constructed, the construction costs still exceeded $36,000. At about $15,000 per mile, the company felt the costs too extravagant for a logging railroad, and construction soon ceased. At best, the line would have been a nominal common carrier, since the county the line was constructed in was sparsely populated.

In August 1892 the Laurel River & Hot Springs Railroad had purchased a new 2-6-0 from Baldwin Locomotive Works. The locomotive arrived the following October with "James Wyman," the name of the railroad's first president, painted on the side. The locomotive remained unnumbered during its short tenure with the railroad. In addition to the locomotive, the company obtained six flatcars.

When the lumber company decided to halt construction, the equipment was stored at the company headquarters at Hot Springs, North Carolina, until

The *James Wyman* was a Baldwin-built 2-6-0 constructed in 1892 on a two foot frame. The locomotive was equipped with 12" × 16" cylinders and 33" drivers. The locomotive was scrapped in 1935. Courtesy of the Railroad Museum of Pennsylvania.

disposal. The locomotive was originally sold to the Wescasset, Waterville & Farmington Railroad. After that railroad could not finance the sale, the locomotive finally ended up on the roster of the Sandy River as its #3, and then on the Sandy River & Rangely Lakes as its #16.

The State Railroad Commissioner's report of 1892 lists the railroad, but it is not listed in the report of 1894.

After the first attempt to build an independent railroad in Madison County failed miserably in 1894, a second attempt originated in Stackhouse, North Carolina, in 1897. This second line was also to be a logging line and would extend from Stackhouse to the Laurel section of the county.

This second attempt was organized on May 8, 1897, by the North Carolina Land and Timber Company. Little progress was recorded due to financial difficulties. In December 1903 the company was forced into bankruptcy after constructing a short section of track out of Stackhouse. Little additional activity took place on this line until 1910.

In 1910 the Madison County Railroad acquired the assets of the Laurel River Logging Company, and construction resumed from Stackhouse to Runion, and then on to Laurel. The railroad also began the process of consolidating the disjointed tracks which existed in the county.

Initial capital was $10,000 in order to facilitate the consolidation of timber reserves. The timber reserves were estimated to be 200,000,000 board feet of processed lumber on 40,000 acres of land. The initial target of the timbering was poplar and pine.

Independent railroad construction had started in 1901 when loggers hauled a 0-4-4 Forney locomotive over the mountain to help log the Pounding Mill area. Teams of oxen and men spent a laborious month trying to drag the locomotive from Greeneville, Tennessee, to Pounding Mill. This operation was organized by Ansin G. Betts, who also set up a band mill at the headwaters of Pounding Mill Creek. His railroad extended from Pounding Mill to the community of Allenstand. The tracks were made of wood rails, implying the operation was not to be permanent.

It took three years for the timbering to be completed around Pounding Mill, and the operation then moved to Little Field. After two years of cutting, the timber around Little Field was depleted. At Little Field, the railroad was extended from the mouth of Pounding Mill to the head of the Little Laurel Creek, near the Tennessee state line.

After the Little Field operation was completed, the small Forney locomotive was used exclusively to either lay track or remove it from previously timbered areas. Since the Forney-type locomotive was not designed for logging service, many of the retired railroad workers remembered that the small locomotive struggled to handle a single car, and occasionally a second loaded car.

For the Madison County Railroad, the right-of-way included a 100-foot swath with the track placed

This small 0-4-4 Forney locomotive was hauled by oxen and men over the mountain from Greeneville, Tennessee. It later served as a backup locomotive for the Madison County Railroad. Collection of Bruce Sprinkle.

in the center of the path. The railroad entered at least two lawsuits in Madison County courts requesting the state's intervention so the right-of-way could be constructed through privately held lands. In order to request the state's condemnation of private property under the right of eminent domain, the railroad had to be listed as a common carrier. The railroad was also listed as a duly chartered corporation in the court documents.

The total length of the line was approximately 30 miles of track. The line eventually stretched from Stackhouse, paralleling the Southern Railway tracks, to Runion, where it turned northward into Madison

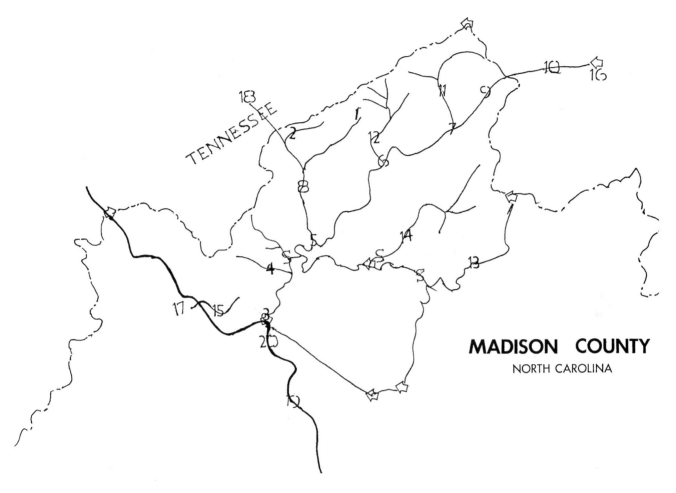

MADISON COUNTY
NORTH CAROLINA

(1) Logging activity began in 1901 when a Forney locomotive was hauled over from Greeneville, Tennessee. (2) Logging activity commenced in Little Fields in 1904. (3) Runion was the location of the failed New England Southern Timber & Land Company (1892), the failed North Carolina Timber & Land Company (1897), and the Laurel River Logging Company, which was organized in 1899. (4) Little Hurricane was the location of Pete McCoy's machine shop. (5) Belva was the location of the Gahagan Cannery and corn mill. (6) Durid was the location of one of the Curry Brothers' band mills. (7) Carmen was the location of a commissary and office for the logging operations. (8) Little Laurel was the location of the Ansin G. Betts lumber yard. (9) A commissary was located at Mill Creek. A 22-foot diameter poplar was also cut near this location. (10) At Flint Creek, a portion of the line extended four miles into Tennessee to Roaring Fork. (11) Big Creek. (12) Hicky Fork was the place where Ansin G. Betts sold the property to the Curry Brothers Lumber Company. (13) Foster's Creek was the location of a splash dam. (14) The railroad ran through Spill Corn and on to the Big Laurel splash dam. (15) The Laurel River & Hot Springs Railroad ran two and a half miles up to Silver Mine from this location. (16) The full extension of the line to Roaring Fork, Tennessee. (17) Hot Springs, North Carolina, was the location of the Hot Springs Inn, a connection with the Southern Railway, and the location of the New England Southern Land & Timber Company's mill in 1892. (18) The route to Greeneville, Tennessee, where the Forney locomotive was hauled over the mountains. (19) The route of the Southern Railway tracks. (20) Stackhouse, the connection between the Southern Railway and the Madison County Railroad. Courtesy of Bruce Sprinkle.

The main motive power on the Madison County Railroad was a three-truck Shay locomotive. Collection of Bruce Sprinkle.

County. Tracks were to eventually extend as far north as Roaring Fork, which is located near Flag Pond, Tennessee. By 1925, most activity on the railroad had ceased. The rails and rolling stock largely stayed on site until the late 1930s, at which time the remaining locomotive and rails were cut up for scrap metal and reportedly sold to Japan.

An interesting development of "what might have been" involved H. S. Howland. Howland was the controlling interest in the Asheville and Craggy Mount Railroad and considered the Madison County Railroad a possible major component of a connecting rail-road between the Southern Railway and the Clinch-field Railroad. The company chartered to facilitate the connection was the Asheville & East Tennessee Railroad. Madison and Yancey counties were each asked to raise $200,000 in order to complete the line from the Southern connection in Madison County to the Clinchfield connection in Yancey County at or near the community of Galax. Both counties came up far short in the raising of bonds, and the project was never attempted.

NORWOOD LUMBER COMPANY AND RAILROAD

Norwood Lumber Company loggers pose with their log loader and Class "A" Climax locomotive near Forney Creek, North Carolina. Collection of Red Haney.

The Norwood Lumber Company of West Virginia proposed on March 3, 1910, to build a logging line in Western North Carolina. The line was to extend up to Forney Creek. The total length of the line would be eight miles, with a connection with the Southern Railway located at Bushnell, North Carolina. This section of track was referred to as the Carolina & Tennessee Southern, a subsidiary of the Southern Railway.

A large mill was projected for construction at Bryson City to facilitate processing of the timber. The lands purchased for timbering had previously belonged to the Harvey Woodbury Company of Bryson City.

Louis Carr was one of the organizers of the Norwood Lumber Company. Carr was also instrumental in founding the Carr Lumber Company in Transylvania County a few years later.

Norwood Lumber Company's railroad extended up Forney Creek to an inclined railroad. From there, it continued on up to the gap between Andrews Bald and Clingman's Dome. From Clingman's Dome it followed a ridge between Noland and Forney Creek.

Norwood's engine roster included a Lima-built Shay, c/n 2418, which they purchased new as their #1. The company also obtained two Class "A" Climax locomotives which both carried the number four. The difference between the two locomotives was that one had a square water tank and the other had a round water tank. The men on the railroad referred to these two locomotives as "Black Satchels."

Table 74—CAROLINA & TENNESSEE SOUTHERN RAILWAY.

W. H. Paxton, General Freight Agent, Atlanta, Ga.
H. F. Cary, General Passenger Agent, Washington, D.C.
G. R. Loyall, General Superintendent, Knoxville, Tenn.

....	No. 121	Ms	*March 21, 1915.*	No. 122	....	.....
....	g1 30 P M	0	lve....Bushnell....arr.	5 30 P M	....	.....
....	1 50 »	3	........Collinwood........	5 05 »	....	.....
....	2 05 »	5	.........Ecola.........	4 50 »	....	.....
....	2 35 »	9	........Marcus.........	4 25 »	....	.....
....	3 00 »	12	.........Ritter	4 10 »	....	.....
....	3 30 P M	14	arr.....**Fontana** ....lve.	g4 00 P M	....	.....

The Carolina & Tennessee Southern was a subsidiary of the Southern Railroad. No motive power was lettered separately for the railroad, and the railroad bed is now under Lake Fontana, North Carolina. Courtesy of *The Official Railway Guide*.

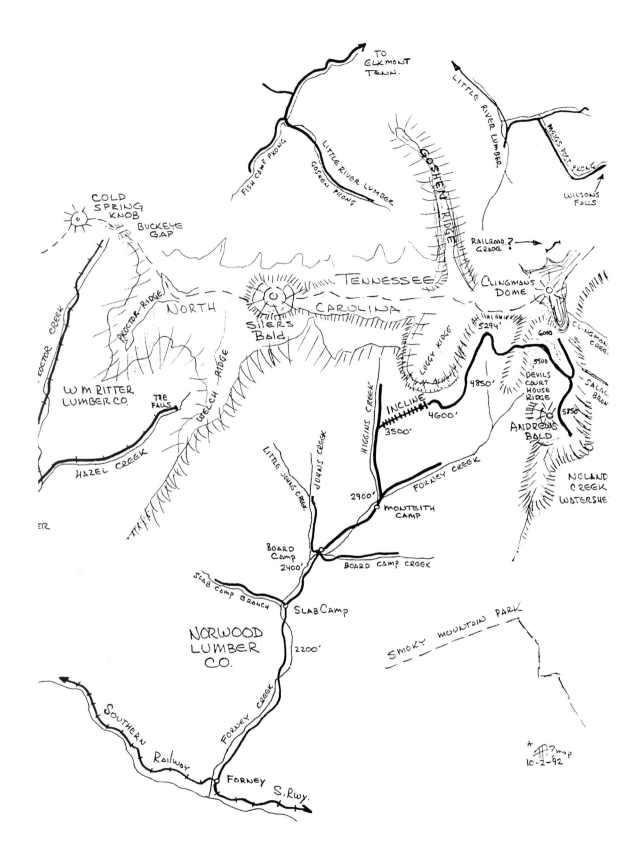

Both Ritter and Forney, North Carolina, served as base operations for narrow gauge logging lines. Ritter serviced the W.M. Ritter Lumber Company line which followed both Proctor and Hazel Creeks. The Norwood Lumber Company connected with the Southern Railway at Forney and ran north, eventually reaching the summit of Andrews Bald at an elevation of 5,580 feet above sea level. Courtesy of Tom Fetters.

Number 4 of the Norwood Lumber Company leads a train of log cars, followed by another Class "A" Climax in the rear, circa 1915. Collection of Red Haney.

A Norwood Lumber Company crew poses with their Class "A" Climax locomotive. The photograph depicts the link and pin coupling system of the locomotive. Collection of Red Haney.

In 1915, two tragic events signaled the end of Norwood's operations. Lewis Ledford, the planing mill supervisor, was killed while trying to change a worn belt on one of the steam-driven planers. Almost two weeks after his death, a fire swept through the dry kiln and mill at Forney, destroying the entire complex. Most of Norwood's employees went on to work for the Blackwood Lumber Company at East La Porte, North Carolina.

In 1929, the 17,000 acres of Norwood's holdings were obtained for inclusion in the Great Smoky Mountains National Park.

The Climax locomotive #4 with the round water tank went to Crusoe, North Carolina, in 1931 and was used on the Powell & Denning Lumber Company Railroad. This line was a disjointed railroad, having no connection with any other railroad, and ran up the east fork of the Pigeon River.

The Carolina & Tennessee Southern track continued to serve the area until 1944, when the line was abandoned due to the flooding of the Little Tennessee River to form Fontana Lake. Prior to its abandonment, the railroad helped to facilitate the construction of the dam.

The dam was so desperately needed to provide electricity for the local area and for a burgeoning aluminum processing industry that the lake was flooded before the rails could be salvaged. When the water is low due to periodic dam inspections, the old rails can still be observed, still in place.

KITCHEN LUMBER COMPANY

Kitchen Lumber Company was headquartered in Ashland, Kentucky, but logged 20,000 acres of hardwood forest in Swain and Graham counties. The majority of the cutting took place between 1920 and 1929. Kitchen was but one of several companies which undertook the task of cutting out the headwaters of the Little Tennessee River on land to be flooded by the construction of four dams by the Aluminum Corporation of American, better known as Alcoa.

The Swain County operation centered around Twenty-mile Creek, where Kitchen built approximately 15 miles of 3' gauge track to its mill on the Little Tennessee River. Lumber was loaded onto a barge which was powered by a homemade steamboat named the *Vivien,* and then moved four miles downstream to Fontana. At Fontana, the lumber was transferred to the Carolina & Tennessee Southern Railroad.

A second Kitchen Lumber Company operation was centered at Topoca, North Carolina. Kitchen was able to utilize Alcoa's own private railroad to conduct several branchline logging operations. In this manner, Kitchen minimized its costs while extracting as much of the hardwood as possible from the area.

Kitchen Lumber Company was one of the few railroads in Western North Carolina to employ the Heisler geared locomotive. In addition to a Climax on its roster, c/n 1517, four Heislers were used. The Heisler construction numbers were 1473, 1485, 1512, and 1531. They were much more accepted with loggers who could operate on flat land and in swampy areas, where little curvature in the track was the normal construction pattern.

Kitchen Lumber Company was one of the few Western North Carolina loggers to utilize Heisler locomotives. The #4, c/n 1473, was constructed in 1923 for a 3' gauge. Salvage operations are under way to place the locomotive back on the track. Collection of Red Haney.

BIBLIOGRAPHY

Bethel Junior High School. *Sunburst: A Story of Champion International Logging Operations on the Upper Pigeon River*. Waynesville, North Carolina, 1978.

Brosnan, D. W. "Selling What Railroads Can Produce." *Progressive Railroading* Jan.-Feb. 1964: 2-6.

Brown, Cecil Kenneth. *A State Movement in the Railroad Development*. Chapel Hill, North Carolina: University of North Carolina at Chapel Hill, 1928.

Bryant, Ralph C. *Logging: The Principles and General Methods of Operation in the U.S.* New York: Wiley & Sons, 1923.

Cannon, William S. "Yancey, Nee Black Mountain," *Trains, the Magazine of Railroading* Aug. 1974: 35-40.

Castner, Charles. "Aboard America's Oldest Active Steamer!" *Family Lines Magazine* Jan.-Feb. 1975: 6-7.

Castner, Charles. "Charles Kuralt Takes Seaboard System's Santa Train 'on the Road.'" *Seaboard System News* Jan.-Feb. 1983.

"Cliffside Railroad." Cone Mill Publication. Internal memo.

"Clinchfield Railroad: A Man-Made Wonder." *Family Lines Magazine* July-August 1980: 17-19.

Clinchfield Railroad, Louisiville, Ky. Family Lines Public Relations Department, 1980.

Davis, Burke. *The Southern Railway: Road of the Innovators*. Chapel Hill, North Carolina: University of North Carolina Press, 1985.

Ferrell, Mallory Hope. "Sidewinders and a Singing Engineer." *Trains* Magazine January 1963.

Ferrell, Mallory Hope. *Tweetsie Country*. Johnson City, Tennessee: The Overmountain Press, 1979.

"Ghost Railroads of Tennessee." *Cocke County Banner*

2 July 1978: 15-20.

Gilbert, John, and Jeffrey Grady. *Crossties Through Carolina*. Raleigh, North Carolina: Helios Press, 1969.

Gilbert, John F. *Crossties Over Saluda*. Raleigh, North Carolina: Crossties Press, 1973.

Goforth, James A. *Building the Clinchfield*. Erwin, Tennessee: Gem Publishers, 1989.

Goforth, James A. *When Steam Ran the Clinchfield*. Erwin, Tennessee: Gem Publishers, 1991.

Harrison, Fairfax. *A Legal History of the Lines of Railroads of the Southern Railway Company*. Washington, DC. 1921.

Harshaw, Lou. *Trains, Trestles and Tunnels*. Lakemont, Georgia: Copple House Books, 1977.

Heisler Locomotive Works. Erie, Pennsylvania. Reprint, 1966.

Hilton, George W. *American Narrow Gauge Railroads*. Stanford, California: Stanford University Press, 1990.

Jones, Bill, and Henry Samples. "Clinchfield Employees Accused of Kickback, Swindling Plots" *Johnson City Press-Chronicle* 20 June 1979.

King, Spencer Bidwell. "Railroads in Western North Carolina." Unpublished master's thesis, Western Carolina University.

King, Steve. *Clinchfield Country*. Silver Springs, Maryland: Old Line Graphics, 1988.

Koch, Michael. *Shay: Titan of the Timber*. Denver: World Press, 1971.

Koch, Michael. *Steam and Thunder in the Timber*. Denver: World Press, 1979.

Krause, John. *American Narrow Gauge*. San Marino, California: Golden West Books, 1978.

Lauterer, Maggie. "Railroad Changed Bee Tree Forever." East Neighbors, *Asheville Citizen-Times* 9 September 1986: 7.

Lonon, J. L. *Tall Tales of the Rails*. Johnson City, Tennessee: The Overmountain Press, 1989.

McBride, H. A. "The Clinchfield Route" *Railroad Magazine* Dec. 1953: 17-33.

McDonald, Garreth M. *A Guide To the Great Smoky Mountain Railway*. Pleasant Garden, North Carolina: The Short Line, 1991.

Official Railway Guide. New York: KIII Information Company, 1892-1947.

P., Andy. "Yes, There Was a Tweetsie." *Avery Journal* 26, September 1991.

Parker, Francis H. "The Yancey Railroad Layout." *Model Railroader* August 1974: 33-39.

Plemmons, Jan C. *Treasures of Toxaway*. Jacksonville, Florida. 1984.

Prince, Richard E. *The L&N Steam Locomotive*. Salt Lake City, Utah: K/P Graphics, 1986.

Prince, Richard E. *The Southern Railway System Steam Locomotives and Boats*. Salt Lake City, Utah: K/P Graphics, 1986.

Rainey, Lee. "The Lawndale Dummy." *The Blue Ridge Stemwinder* Fall 1991: 3-11.

Reid, H. *Clinchfield's Old #5, Now #1 Attraction*. Richmond, Virginia: Old Dominion Chapter, NHRS, 1972.

Reid, H. *Extra South*. Trenton, New Jersey: Carstens Publications, 1986.

Robertson, Archie. *Slow Train to Yesterday*. Boston: Houghton Mifflin, 1945.

Robertson, Reuben B. "Three Captains, Three Churches." Personal interview on file with the Canton Area Historical Museum.

Scheer, Julian, and Elizabeth M. Black. *Tweetsie*. 1958. Johnson City, Tennessee: The Overmountain Press, 1991.

Shaffer, Frank. "Here Comes Clinchfield." *Trains* Magazine Milwaukee, Wisconsin: Kalmbach Publishing, August 1961: 30-38.

Sink, Tom L., and Paul K. Withers. *Southern: A Motive Power Pictorial*. Hatfield, Pennsylvania: Crusader Printing, 1987.

Southern Railway Standards of the Department of Maintenance of Way and Structures. Vol 1. Spencer, North Carolina: Southern Railway Historical Association, 1989.

Sulzer, Elmer. *Ghost Railroads of Tennessee*. Indianapolis, Indiana: Vaine A. Jones Company, 1975.

Train Shay Cyclopedia: Shays and Other Geared Locomotives. Novato, California: Newton K. Gregg, Publisher, 1975.

Trelease, Allen W. *The North Carolina Railroad, 1849-1871, and the Modernization of North Carolina*. Chapel Hill, North Carolina, 1991.

Van Hoppen, Iva, and John J. Van Hoppen. *Western North Carolina Since the Civil War*. Boone, North Carolina: Appalachian Consortium, 1973.

Weals, Vic. *Last Train to Elkmont*. Knoxville, Tennessee: Olden Press, 1991.

Webb, William. *The Southern Railway System: An Illustrated History*. Erin, Ontario, Canada: Boston Mills Press, 1986.

Westveer, Brian. *Railroad Crossings of the Blue Ridge*. Little Switzerland, North Carolina: Memories Publishing, 1990.

Westveer, Brian. "Railroads Above the Toes." *The Idyll* Spring 1990: 7.

Westveer, Brian. *Tweetsie Country—Following the Roadbed*. Little Switzerland, North Carolina: Memories Publishing, 1984.

Wiley, Aubrey, and Conley Wallace. *The Southern Railway Handbook*. Goode, Virginia: W-W Publications, 1983.

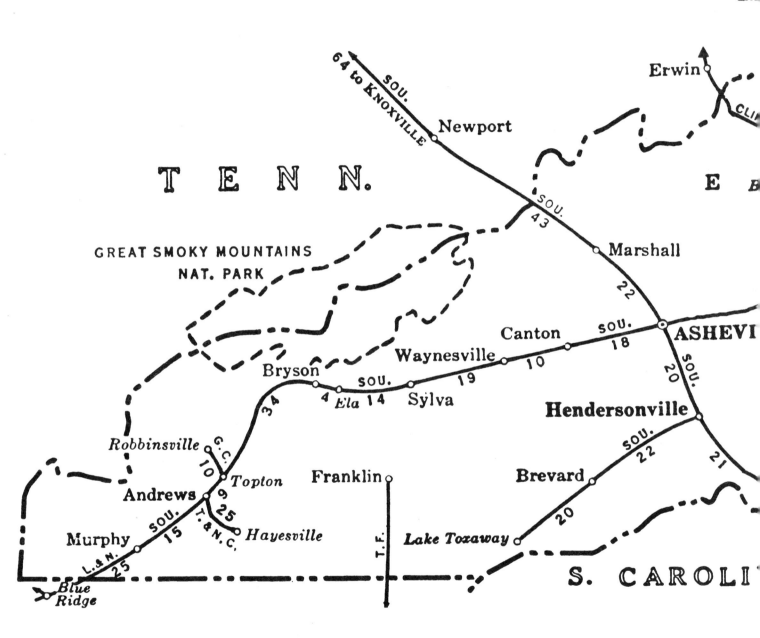

WESTERN PORTION
OF
NORTH CAROLINA